D1265205

THE KUOMINTANG DEBACLE OF 1949

Conquest or Collapse?

Other volumes in preparation

PROBLEMS IN ASIAN CIVILIZATIONS

THE KUOMINTANG
DEBACLE OF 1949

Conquest or Collapse?

EDITED WITH AN INTRODUCTION BY

Pichon P. Y. Loh

UPSALA COLLEGE

D. C. HEATH AND COMPANY · BOSTON

Library of Congress Catalog Card Number 64-8154

COPYRIGHT © 1965 BY D. C. HEATH AND COMPANY

BOSTON   INDIANAPOLIS   CHICAGO   DALLAS   SAN FRANCISCO   ATLANTA

Table of Contents

Introduction

THE debacle of the Kuomintang on the mainland of China has been the topic of a heated debate in America since that fateful year of 1949, and will doubtless remain for some time a subject for careful study by interested scholars. To many an observer, the debacle symbolizes the end of an old, if not honored, tradition and the advent of a new, if not Western one. To others, it has been difficult to believe that history could have wrought so much upheaval in four brief years following the conclusion of the Second World War to a nation so rich in tradition and so abounding in prospect. Either out of a belief in the "fundamental Chinese personality and culture" or out of a conviction in the ultimate triumph of the good, the latter have refused to accept the debacle of the Kuomintang except as a passing phenomenon, a bad dream. Hence, the missionary-diplomat John Leighton Stuart, whose useful commentary on the Kuomintang government is among the selections in this volume, expressed his prayerful hope in the following terms: "I have faith that *somehow* and within a not very long time this monstrous evil will have run its course, and, having been weighed and found wanting, will be forced to relax its grip and be gone." [1] Yet, the Chinese Communist government, inaugurated on October 1, 1949, has remained in power and the return of the Kuomintang to the mainland has been little more than a matter of uncertain speculation.

This study deals primarily with the factors contributing to the fall of the Kuomintang rather than those leading to the eventual victory of the Chinese Communist Party. While the two aspects of this historical process are closely interrelated, they may for analytical purpose be treated as separate problems for investigation. To be sure, an adequate understanding of the character of the Chinese revolution cannot be gained without attention to the whole, but the vastly complex nature of the revolution also requires an analysis of its parts. Moreover, if the view is correct that the Kuomintang failed largely by default and the Chinese Communist Party in a large sense moved into a political vacuum, the emphasis on one aspect of the Chinese revolution is amply justified.

Whatever else may be said about the political contest between the two parties, consensus exists that the final outcome of the power struggle was decided by military forces. It was a clear case of military defeat of one party by another. But, if the prowess of the Communist forces accounted for the speed with which the Communist takeover of the mainland was consummated, it could hardly be adduced as a satisfactory explanation of the political effectiveness of the Communist Party. And if the Communist program undergirded the strength and appeal of the party, the supplantation of the Kuomintang as the ruling power could not be explained simply in terms of the efficacy of the Communist program. Consideration of the causes of the Kuomintang debacle requires the consideration of a number of other factors and evokes a host of related issues.

The overriding question, as the selections in this volume will suggest, remains whether the fall of the Kuomintang in the

[1] Italics added.

manner and at the time it did is historically inevitable or whether it is principally the result of a combination of human frailties and contrivances. Is the Kuomintang debacle, in other words, to be attributed to political factors that could have been avoided or at least mitigated, or to natural historical forces that are well beyond reasonable limits of expectation and political control? The question of general concern, then, is the familiar one of Hero and History, of the interplay of historical forces and human factors, carrying as they do the manifold implications of principle, policy, program and practice.

The sources in this volume are selected, in the main, for the rationally compelling interpretations they evince on the major positions taken on this subject. If some are regarded as falling short of the expected level of rationality, they at least contain a high degree of internal consistency and represent significant, if also controversial, viewpoints. The first selection, by Professor A. Doak Barnett, is an overall assessment of various factors contributing to the decline of the Kuomintang, which underscores at the same time the devastating effect of the Second World War on an already highly explosive situation. This essay, appearing in 1963, also provides a balanced historical frame of reference for the other selections classified into five sections. The selections in the first section explain the Kuomintang debacle in terms of the immediate events of the civil war period, stressing the military factor and the question of liaison between the government and the people in the midst of worsening conditions and mounting tensions. The second section discusses the proximate events of the Second World War that began, for China, in 1937, and finds in the war against Japan the roots of the deteriorating political, social and economic conditions that grew into dangerous proportions during the civil war period. The selections in the third section, seeking long-range causes, identify the weaknesses of the Kuomintang in the program and policy of the party and

the political framework of its operation since its accession to national power in 1928. Others, in the fourth section, focus their attention on the international aspect of the Chinese civil strife, adverting to Communist conspiratorial activities originated from the Soviet Union since the Bolshevik revolution of 1917 and to the role of America during this period. Still others, in the fifth section, view the Kuomintang debacle within the broad scope of the dynamics of history, specifically raising questions of the character of the Kuomintang movement and of the inevitability of its collapse.

As analysts of the immediate events, F. F. Liu, once a Kuomintang army officer, and Professor Michael Lindsay, for four years an observer of the Communist 18th Group Army, center their attention on the military aspect of the civil strife of 1945–49. It should be noted, however, that in drawing upon their firsthand knowledge of the Chinese armed forces, they do so with perspective. Liu, in discussing the Kuomintang military power and posture, attributes the fall of his party to organizational flaws and strategic errors and, like Barnett, to the eight years of war against Japan that had overtaxed the government. Lindsay, more conversant with Communist military strengths than with Kuomintang military weaknesses, lays stress on the Communist use of "special organization and fighting method to compensate for its tremendous inferiority in equipment." His prognosis of the decisive importance of psychological warfare to sway the allegiance of enemy troops has been fully borne out by the course of events in 1948–49.

John Leighton Stuart, educator and diplomat, ascribed the Kuomintang's failure more to poor public relations after 1945 than to deficient public programs. He regarded Chiang as being in possession of a progressive frame of mind and the Kuomintang policy as being essentially sound and democratic. Therefore, while many of his diplomatic associates urged Chiang to undertake basic democratic reforms in cooperation with the "liberal" leaders, Stuart advised that Chiang lead a new revolutionary movement "with something of the adventurous enthusiasm" of the 1920's that would draw into the Kuomintang orbit the students and younger intellectuals as volunteer propagandists for the party.

The effect of the Second World War is stressed by Professor Edwin O. Reischauer. He recognizes the political weaknesses of the Kuomintang, but he ascribes its fall to historical forces beyond the control of the party, namely, the impact of the war against Japan and the stupendousness of the task of modernization in a country as vast and as complex as China. Chang Kia-ngau, an official of long standing in economic affairs, believes that the war created unfavorable, but not impossible, conditions. He points to serious errors in government economic policy and management, deploring at the same time the government's inability, among other things, to integrate the rural and urban sectors of the nation's economy. According to him, the government showed neither fortitude nor foresight in failing to effect basic fiscal reforms on three propitious moments during and immediately after the Second World War, in 1938–39, 1941 and 1945.

John S. Service, an American Foreign Service Officer, was a close observer of the Chinese scene after the outbreak of war with Japan. As an ardent believer in political liberalism, he is deeply concerned with the lack of social consciousness and political action on the part of the Kuomintang leaders. Kuomintang China, in his view, was in dire need of immediate reform, but he questions whether the Kuomintang, so much weighed down by its conservative outlook and selfish interest, was able to deal constructively with the pressing political, social and economic issues. He offers as a solution the formation of a liberal government without reference to Chiang.

Moving to explanations of more general positions, we may refer to a number of views that the Kuomintang's own faults account for its fall. Professor Tang Tsou points to the glaring discrepancy between the avowed objectives of the party and the actual state of affairs. As he sees it, the Three People's Principles — Nationalism, Democracy, and People's Livelihood — received little more than verbal attention from the Kuomintang after it inherited the mantle of national power in 1928.

Carsun Chang, a noted third party leader strongly predisposed to political pluralism, sees the fundamental weakness of the Kuomintang in the inherent defectiveness of tutelary government. What China needs, he avers, is democratic constitutionalism and responsible party government. But democracy cannot be taught; it has to be lived. To try to teach democracy, as the Kuomintang said it would, is futile at best. Professor Ch'ien Tuan-sheng agrees with Carsun Chang that what ails China's body social is her defective body politic, but he ascribes the reason for the Kuomintang's dictatorship not to the inherent contradiction of tutelage, but to the innate inability of military rule to become democratic. The Kuomintang, in Ch'ien's opinion, has never really advanced beyond the first stage of military government as envisaged by Sun Yat-sen.

To General Albert C. Wedemeyer, the civil war in China was in effect a Sino-Soviet war. For the result of this conflict, the American government must also be held accountable to the extent that it failed to identify the issues at hand and adopt a "realistic approach" to the situation in the Far East. In regard to China's domestic politics, he agrees with Stuart that Chiang, a democrat at heart, was compelled by force of circumstances to impose a measure of dictatorship, which, unfortunately, did nothing to endear him to his people. But here the two part ways. China, Wedemeyer argues, needs not more democracy, but more authority, the lack of which is the root cause of the weakness and failure of the Kuomintang.

Professor Ping-chia Kuo singles out land reform as basic to social stability in China.

Without specific reference to political system or form, he states that government power must be anchored in the ability and readiness of the government to satisfy the "basic needs" of the eighty percent of the Chinese people who work the land. This, Kuo observes, the Kuomintang government failed to do during the twenty years of its rule on the mainland.

The degree and nature of foreign involvement and responsibility is a subject of major concern for many persons. Hu Shih, onetime Chinese Ambassador to the U. S. and Chancellor of the National Peking University, considered the exportation of revolution from the Soviet Union as characteristic of the international communist movement of his time. He regarded the Communist revolutions in China and East Europe equally the product of the same master plan designed in its essentials and guided in its execution by Stalin. Professor Anthony Kubek, a student of the "isolationist" Professor Charles Callan Tansill, concurs in his 1963 publication in Hu's depiction of the conspiratorial nature of international communism, but he is equally disturbed over what he considers to be America's inexcusable failure to uphold the banner of freedom in China.

Dean Acheson, American Secretary of State at the time of the Kuomintang debacle, admits America's involvement in China in an effort to influence the trend of events, but he firmly denies the allegation that the secret Yalta Agreement of February 1945 between the U. S., Britain, and the Soviet Union was an act of appeasement to the latter. The Yalta Agreement, argues Acheson, was neither a betrayal of moral principles nor a surrender of the basic national interests of China or America. It was a political decision dictated by military considerations and did not alter the balance of China's domestic forces. The China problem, in any event, is a Chinese problem requiring domestic solution, for its roots are deep in the issues that have faced the nation at least since the mid-nineteenth century. Whereas

Kubek thinks it possible to avert the Kuomintang debacle by decisive and timely American action, Acheson says that "nothing that this country did or could have done within the reasonable limits of its capabilities could have changed that result."

Chiang Kai-shek's reflections on the rise and fall of the Kuomintang are revealing if also tendentious. While he has no doubt of the Soviet origin of Chinese Communism and of the international responsibility of the U. S., he is of the view that the causes of the fall of his government on the mainland must be sought in China itself. He explains his government's critical errors in policy and strategy as well as in organization and technique. The Kuomintang as a party, he says, was too slow in perceiving the true nature of Chinese Communism and, having perceived, was too irresolute in its suppression.

Some commentators, placing political events in the stream of history, give emphasis to the logic and dynamics of history. Professor Charles P. Fitzgerald, shares many of the views of the others. He believes (with Liu, Service and Carsun Chang) that the Kuomintang was weakened by corruption and nepotism, (with Kuo and Fairbank) that it defaulted on social reforms, and (with Lindsay and Stuart) that it failed to capture the imagination of the people. But Fitzgerald also believes that one needs to place the history of the Kuomintang in the context of the Chinese dynastic spiral in order to grasp fully the nature and causes of its debacle. The Kuomintang, described as being in the tradition of the late nineteenth-century reform movement, is said to have lost its identity with China's cultural heritage without having in the meantime attained a new identity with Western culture. Having lost its identity, the Kuomintang loses itself in history. The Communist victory, on the other hand, is characterized as a return to China's traditional pattern of rule and the completion of another dynastic cycle.

In contrast with Fitzgerald's cyclical

theory is Mao Tse-tung's theory of uni-linear progression. Mao, in the tradition of Leninism-Stalinism, posits that history moves inexorably forward from epoch to epoch to the realization of the classless society and that the logic of history is applicable to China no less than to other countries. Without stating it explicitly (for the article from which the selection is excerpted first appeared in 1939), Mao relegates the Kuomintang to the historical background as a link between the past and the future, while asserting the historic role the Communists are destined to perform in making a timeless contribution to humanity. The interpretation of the Chinese revolution as presented in *Voprosy Istorii,* a Soviet historical journal, in the article by G. Astafyev, reflects, in general, the Stalinist-Maoist thesis. It does, however, make a strong case, as should surprise no one, to place the Chinese revolution in the context of world revolution, in which the primacy of the Soviet Union and the leadership of Stalin are made abundantly clear.

Professor John K. Fairbank considers several factors leading to the Kuomintang decline, some of them working to overwhelm the party, such as the social upheaval wrought by the peasant upsurge, popular patriotic aspirations, and Communist ideological impact; and others deriving from the weaknesses of the party itself, such as the distrust which the Kuomintang, owing to its cultural and socio-economic conservatism, had of mass movements. He discusses the interplay of personal and impersonal forces confronting the Kuomintang, but advises against uncritical acceptance of theories of historical inevitability.

As the foregoing introduction has shown, the Kuomintang debacle has been debated on three levels: the national level as the product of internal forces, the international level as an acute manifestation of world power struggle, and the universal level as an example of moral ambiguities. Whatever one's persuasion and judgment may be, it is hoped that the selections and their organization will not only bring focus to the bewildering complex of Chinese politics in the immediate post-World War II years but equally evoke broader issues of power and value in the world setting.

In this connection, the selections suggest a number of questions that lend themselves to class discussion, relative to the four principals of the political strife in China: the Kuomintang, the Chinese Communist Party, the Soviet Union, and the United States. In its Kuomintang aspect, one could ask what accounted for the party's failure to take advantage of its enormous popularity during the four eventful years after 1945 to win the students to its side. What could have been done to conciliate the third parties and to prevent the majority of the third-party and non-party leaders from going over to the Communists? What did the government do, or fail to do, to ameliorate the economic plight of the nation? Given the war conditions, could industrialization have been hastened, production increased, and spiraling inflation averted? Could farm reforms have been instituted and implemented, tax structure streamlined, revenue collection made more effective, and government budget balanced? Was the failure of the Kuomintang due primarily to inept ideology, erroneous policy, unrealistic program, inefficient administration, or defective propaganda? Furthermore, one could raise the question whether Chiang Kai-shek is a progressive caught in a difficult age or whether he is a conservative unable to adapt himself to the requirements of modern times. Is he a dictator imposing his personal whims on a politically awakening people, or a democrat living in a time that demands absolute and decisive action? When he fails after more than twenty years of almost uninterrupted public service on the mainland, does he fail his country, or does history fail him?

In the Chinese Communist aspect of the political struggle, questions concerning the setting of the Communist system may be raised in reference to the selection by Mao. While it seems clear, after the events have long occurred, that the leading Chinese Communists were dedicated (and "pure") Communists, was the true nature of Chinese Communism readily discernible or deducible at the time when history was still being made and lived? In retrospect, we can, with logical clarity, state that the modest agrarian programs and moderate political reforms of the Yenan days were the result of a particular revolutionary experience, painfully but wisely learned, that they were put forth and implemented as the most efficacious policy at a given historical stage, and that they in no way contradicted, or deflected from, the professed goal of communism. But was this line of thinking clear and incontrovertible at the time when the Communist leadership counselled prudence and prescribed moderation? Instead of saying that the moderate party line was dialectically applied as an intermediate step leading to the totalitarian dictatorship of the Communist Party, could it not be plausibly argued, given the knowledge, experience and hopes of the time, that Marxist-Leninist dogmas were dialectically professed to justify, under a different political caption, the existence of an essentially "Chinese" party bent on seizing political power?

Moreover, to what degree was the Chinese civil war an extension of the cold war in a bipolarized world? What was the role of the Soviet Union during this period? Did she have a carefully planned strategy for the Chinese revolution, or did she rather feel her way through the labyrinths of world politics and make the most of a rapidly evolving situation in China? How did the Yalta Agreement and the subsequent entry of Soviet troops into Manchuria affect the final outcome in China? What is one to make of the Sino-Soviet Treaty of Friendship and Alliance of August 14, 1945, by which the Soviet Government pledged exclusive moral and material support to the National Government of China? And when Stalin laugh-

ingly characterized his Chinese comrades as radish Communists — red outside and white inside — what precisely did he mean by that? Was it simply another bad joke of poor taste typical of Stalin's cynicism; was it actually intended to be traducing of the "reformist" Chinese Communist Party; or was it meant to confuse and mislead the West?

America's role was of importance. Assuming the national interest of the U. S. in the maintenance of peace in the Far East in general and China in particular, did the objective conditions there permit of the maintenance of peace and security at the same time? Granted the American hope for a reform "coalition government" tilted in favor of the Kuomintang, did the U. S. pursue a course of action consistent with the desired objective? Was the Kuomintang debacle proof of the correctness of George C. Marshall's charges that the Kuomintang generals were guilty of unrealistic assessment of the state of military affairs, or was it rather proof of the incorrectness of the Marshall policy of coalition government that might have cost the Kuomintang invaluable time in launching an early all-out offensive against the Communist? In short, what did America fail to do, if it failed at all? What, if anything, could America have done to reverse or arrest the decline of the Kuomintang government in 1945–49?

These and many other questions are raised directly or inferentially in the selections, in elaboration of the fundamental problems surrounding the debacle of the Kuomintang. But transcending these manifold issues is the overriding question of the inevitability of the Kuomintang debacle. Did historical forces exceed human limits in this instance, or could the Kuomintang debacle of 1949 have been avoided? This central question will surely occupy the attention of scholars and laymen alike for many years to come.

The Conflict of Opinion

"The prolonged Sino-Japanese conflict, which lasted altogether for eight years, had a shattering effect upon China. It was during this period that the process of social disintegration which was to lead ultimately to the collapse of the Nationalist regime began."

— A. Doak Barnett

"He [Chiang Kai-shek] recognized the real nature of the Chinese Communists before almost any others of his fellow countrymen or of Americans . . . living in China, and he resolutely decided to risk misunderstanding, unpopularity and even defeat in following out his own better comprehension of this crucial issue."

— John Leighton Stuart

"His [Chiang Kai-shek's] unbounded confidence in his political and military judgment, his faith in his infallibility, and his mystic sense of identity with the nation made him arrogant and unsusceptible to advice and argument. . . . Thus, the seeds of his downfall were imbedded in the amazing political skill which had given him his earlier successes."

— Tang Tsou

"China's real need was for a government with the power to govern. . . . The powers of the Chinese Nationalist Government, far from being totalitarian, were much too limited. It interfered with the individual too little, not too much. Its sins of omission, not of commission, were the cause of its eventual downfall."

— Albert C. Wedemeyer

"The immediate underlying factor in the Communist rise to power was the Kuomintang's failure to lead the country in a program of creative action. . . . Intent on holding power, it distrusted the enthusiasm of private agencies and individuals. It feared change in a rapidly changing world. Its failure in political leadership gave the Communists an opportunity which they otherwise might not have had."

— John K. Fairbank

"From all available evidences, the Kuomintang had a great opportunity to put land reform into effect. . . . But the groups in control were opposed to social change. Without social change there could be no improvement in the standard of living of the people. This was the fatal weakness of the Kuomintang government."

— Ping-chia Kuo

"Economic instability finally led to a general loss of confidence in the Nationalist government, and total collapse of political and social morals followed. Into this chaos and political and moral vacuum almost any militant group promising a clear sweep could have moved without strong opposition; and the Communists were there to take full advantage of the situation."

— Chang Kia-ngau

". . . The Chinese Communist Party, partly by design and partly by extraordinary historical circumstances, has possessed a formidable army of its own almost from the very early years of its founding. . . . This unique feature of the Chinese Communist Party has been the most important source of its strength, which Stalin, the masterful strategist of world Communism, has been able to nurture, support, and in the course of 25 years develop into a most powerful instrumentality for subjugating China and thereby dominating the whole Asiatic continent."

— Hu Shih

"The unfortunate but inescapable fact is that the ominous result of the civil war in China was beyond the control of the government of the United States. . . . It was the product of internal Chinese forces, forces which this country tried to influence but could not."

— Dean Acheson

". . . The Chinese revolution taken as a whole involves a twofold task. That is to say, it embraces a revolution that is bourgeois-democratic in character (a new-democratic revolution) and a revolution that is proletarian-socialist in character. . . . The leadership in this twofold revolutionary task rests on the shoulders of the party of the Chinese proletariat, the Chinese Communist Party, for without its leadership no revolution can succeed."

— Mao Tse-tung

"When the war ended the Communists resorted to armed insurrection. They did everything to nullify all reconstruction projects, to hinder the Government's program of demobilization, to disrupt the nation's economic life and to upset its social order. They spread national defeatism at a time when the people were weary after the long war. Finally, the general public became so confused and bewildered that all that they asked was peace at any cost, however transient it might turn out to be. This was the basic reason for the tragic reverses which China suffered in her war against Communism."

— Chiang Kai-shek

PROBLEMS AND ISSUES

Multiple Factors

A. DOAK BARNETT

Professor Barnett, Professor of Government at Columbia University and Chairman of the Communist China Studies Committee of its East Asian Institute, is the author of *Communist China and Asia* (1960) and *Communist China: The Early Years, 1949–55* (1964). His on-the-spot reports, written in 1947–49 and published in book form in 1963, clarify many of the basic issues and factors conditioning the Kuomintang defeat and Communist victory. In his introduction to this volume, reproduced below, Professor Barnett is careful to point out the personal and impersonal forces confronting the Chinese nation. Moving through the various levels of causality, he identifies these forces and factors as being the intense revolutionary process of change in values and institutions, national disunity and military regionalism, the Kuomintang's internal division and lack of effective long-range program, the Chinese Communist revolt, the crushing impact of the Second World War, Soviet and American interests in China, economic disintegration and psychological fermentation after the war, and deterioration of morale among the Kuomintang troops.

For decades, one of the most extensive revolutions in history has been taking place in China. Like all great political and social upheavals, it has involved both the emergence of powerful new forces and the collapse of an old order, and it has gone through several distinctive stages. . . .

Whenever a new revolutionary group moves to the center of the stage, it inevitably dominates the scene, and the past tends to fade into obscurity. Subsequently, the new revolutionary leaders propagate the myth that their successes have been due solely to their own omniscience and omnipotence, rather than to the failures and weaknesses of their predecessors. Generally, however, a collapse of the old order is an essential prerequisite to the success of any major revolutionary movement. In China, this collapse was so thorough that by 1949

the Communists were able to take over the country with ease. In a sense, they simply moved into a vacuum.

Although the political disintegration and social chaos that enabled the Communists to seize power in China reached their climax in the years just prior to 1949, one must bear in mind that the Chinese revolution had gone through many different stages before that time — and will doubtless go through others in the future.

Throughout the modern period, China has been engaged in an intense and painful revolutionary process. In fact, the decay of its traditional society and political structure can be dated to the middle of the nineteenth century, when it first encountered a combination of disruptive foreign influences and serious domestic crises. In the half-century that followed, the old order

A. Doak Barnett, *China on the Eve of Communist Takeover* (New York: Frederick A. Praeger, Inc., 1963), pp. 5–13. Reprinted by permission.

1

was slowly undermined, and the Chinese people groped toward new values and institutions.

During the early years of this century, a movement led by Sun Yat-Sen — one that was eventually to become the Chinese Nationalist Party, or Kuomintang — emerged as the most important revolutionary force in the country, but the collapse of the old Manchu Dynasty proceeded even more rapidly than the growth of this new movement. When the old regime toppled in 1911, therefore, there was really nothing to move into the vacuum. As a result, China literally fell apart, and for almost two decades the Central Government in Peking controlled only small portions of the country, while great areas were ruled by local warlords.

The Nationalists continued to develop their political movement, however, and by the 1920's they had become the primary focus of hope for those who yearned for national reunification, political modernization, and economic development. As their strength grew, they slowly acquired the basis for attempting another political revolution. Under the leadership first of Sun Yat-sen and subsequently of Chiang K'ai-shek, and with the support of the small Chinese Communist Party (founded in 1921), they proceeded in the late 1920's to overthrow China's weak Central Government and were able to bring some of the local warlords under control and to establish a new national government in Nanking in 1927–28.

Following the Nationalists' takeover, the first decade of their rule — up until the outbreak of the Sino-Japanese War — was a period of considerable progress and hope. The new regime started to modernize the country. It introduced some moderate social reforms. And it took initial steps toward fostering economic development.

Even in this period, however, the Nationalists encountered serious problems, and they were not able to go very far either in implementing reforms or in solving the most basic and urgent problems confronting the country.

One of their problems was created by the nature of the Nationalist movement itself. From the start, it was composed of heterogeneous, conflicting interests and was hampered by internal divisions that made it difficult either to adopt clear-cut policies or to implement them vigorously. Moreover, it lacked the strength to overcome the remnants of political and military regionalism in China or to impose its will on traditional vested interests in either the countryside or cities. In many local areas of the country, regimes of a warlord sort persisted, blocking genuine national reunification. In the countryside, conservative landlords obstructed the implementation of reforms that were urgently needed to cope with China's fundamental economic problems — problems created by a rapidly growing population and a serious shortage of agricultural land. Within the Nationalist Party itself, factionalism and old-fashioned clique politics sapped the vitality and discipline that the Party's leaders were attempting to create.

Another challenge that faced the Nationalists from the start was posed by domestic Communist revolt. In 1927, the Nationalist-Communist alliance (which had been formed in 1923) split apart. The Nationalists thereupon attempted to crush the Communist movement, but they were unsuccessful, and the Communists went into open insurrection. Even though the strength of the Chinese Communist Party was still small at that time, the Party was able to establish a geographical base for revolution in east-central China (as the Nationalists themselves had done in the south in the early 1920's), to mobilize peasants within this rural area to form a revolutionary guerrilla army, and to start its protracted armed struggle for power. In the early 1930's, the Nationalists mounted several major military campaigns in an attempt to defeat the Communists — campaigns that constituted a significant drain on their resources and energies — but they were never able to destroy the Communist forces completely or to prevent them from retaining a foothold in the countryside.

In the mid-1930's, after they had been forced to retreat to an isolated area in northwest China, the Communists were not, it is true, yet a very formidable immediate threat; but they continued to hold together a revolutionary movement possessing a guerrilla army and a definite geographical base of operations, they had been greatly toughened by their difficult struggle, and they had gained valuable experience in revolutionary techniques. Whether, if China had enjoyed relative stability for several years, the Communists would ever have been able to put this experience to such use that they could present a major threat to the Nationalists is difficult to guess. The tragic fact, however, is that China's brief period of relative stability under the Nationalists was destroyed by Japanese aggression in the 1930's, and the resulting Sino-Japanese War not only struck at the foundations of the Nationalist regime, but also presented unprecedented opportunities for the Communists to pursue their evolving strategy of protracted guerrilla warfare.

Actually, the threat of Japanese aggression was the greatest single problem facing the Nationalists almost from the day they assumed power. Since 1894, the Japanese had made one encroachment after another on China's territory and sovereign rights, and, as they saw China beginning to make some progress toward reunification and modernization, they stepped up the pressure. In 1931–32, they seized Manchuria, one of China's richest regions, and established a Japanese-controlled regime there. Subsequently, they steadily extended their interference and penetration throughout north China. Finally, in 1937, they initiated a major undeclared war against the Nationalist regime, one which soon developed into a full-scale military conflict that

was ultimately to merge with World War II.

The prolonged Sino-Japanese conflict, which lasted altogether for eight years, had a shattering effect upon China. It was during this period that the process of social disintegration which was to lead ultimately to the collapse of the Nationalist regime began. Much of China, including the major urban areas which had been the main sources of the Nationalists' strength, fell into Japanese hands, and the military struggle imposed an intolerable strain on the restricted areas that the Nationalists were able to retain. Forced into backward, isolated, interior regions, the Chinese government had to struggle hard, under the most difficult conditions, simply to survive. Conservative and reactionary forces reasserted their power and influence. Instead of pushing forward with needed reforms, the Nationalists postponed them indefinitely, and resorted increasingly to repressive controls. The economy, subjected to excessive burdens, began to weaken. Inflation reached dangerous proportions, threatening the very foundations of stability. China's intellectuals and students — its modernized and educated elite — became increasingly disillusioned and bitter. Morale and discipline within the Nationalist bureaucracy itself — within the Party, government, and army — were steadily undermined. Cynicism, corruption, and mismanagement grew to serious proportions. Somehow, things held together, and many people clung to the hope that the end of the war would bring not only peace but revitalization. But even before the war had ended, the Nationalists had been gravely weakened by internal decay, and victory in 1945 had a hollow ring.

By contrast, the Sino-Japanese conflict presented the Chinese Communists with unprecedented opportunities to increase their revolutionary strength, and they exploited the wartime situation to the full to enhance their power and influence. In the name of nationalism and patriotism, they formed a second short-lived alliance (or perhaps it should be called a temporary truce) with the Nationalists. By developing successful guerrilla warfare against the Japanese, they were able both to build up their military forces and to exert a considerable appeal to Chinese patriotism. Departing from many of the more extreme revolutionary policies that they had pursued earlier — and were to pursue again later — they implemented in the rural areas under their control a relatively mild land-reform program which created in the minds of many Chinese the image of Communism as a moderate reform movement — an image that was not entirely dispelled until some time after the Communists had achieved power and had begun to put into effect new and drastic revolutionary programs. During the war, as many Chinese intellectuals became progressively disillusioned with the Nationalists, more than a few were attracted by the Communists' general program, innocuously labeled "new democracy" during that period. Most important of all, the Communist movement itself rapidly increased in size and strength. By the end of the war, the Communists controlled and governed most of rural north China — apart from the cities and railways held by the Japanese — and had built up a party of over a million and a revolutionary army of comparable size. They were immeasurably better prepared, in short, than they had been eight years earlier to pursue their struggle for power.

Although the internal balance of power in China between the Nationalists and the Communists had shifted substantially during the war, in purely military terms the Nationalists still had a great preponderance of power — i.e., of men and matériel — in 1945. Both sides were, not surprisingly, highly suspicious of the intentions of the other, and, even before the war had ended, they had begun to jockey for position, preparing for possible civil war. This jockeying continued immediately after the war. With American assistance, Nationalist troops moved rapidly to take over the major cities and rail lines that had been held by the Japanese. The Communists quickly moved some of their best troops into Manchuria, which had been occupied by the Russians during the last few days of the war, and there, with the help of the Russians, they were able to seize substantial stocks of Japanese military equipment.

Yet, despite the intense hostility existing between the Nationalists and Communists, both sides — with American encouragement — were at least willing to talk peace and compromise. There was great war-weariness in China, and a widespread recognition that full-scale civil war would be a major tragedy for the country. The Nationalists were not unaware, in view of their earlier failures to defeat the Communists' guerrilla forces, that full-scale civil war would be a prolonged and difficult struggle and that, if it occurred, China, already seriously weakened by almost a decade of warfare, would encounter enormous difficulties in achieving the hoped-for postwar recovery. The Communists seemed to believe that outright civil war would involve undesirable costs and risks for them, and that they could continue their struggle, and make gains, by other means. Also, the Russians apparently underestimated the seriousness of Nationalist weaknesses and did not believe the Communists could easily achieve military success in China at that time; although the Chinese Communists had greater confidence in themselves, they, too, may well have believed that a full-scale military conflict with the Nationalists could not be won quickly or easily — as it was, in fact, not long thereafter.

This was the context in which the United States Government made a major effort, soon after the war, to mediate the Nationalist-Communist conflict and to prevent the outbreak of civil war. Actually, such efforts had started during the latter stages of the war, the aim then being to bolster China's position in the fighting against Japan. After the war, the American aim was to prevent the outbreak of major civil war in China and to encourage the reunification of the country by peaceful means.

However, the mediation mission of General George C. Marshall proved to be a failure. Whether it ever had any real chance of success is a question that will doubtless be debated for many years to come, as will the question of whether the Nationalist regime might have been able to survive on the mainland if it had obtained a significant breathing spell after the war in which to try to revitalize itself and cope with some of China's most urgent problems. But no peace or breathing spell was possible. The hostility and suspicion between the Nationalists and Communists were so great that even the temporary truce arranged by Marshall broke down in mid-1946, and open civil war erupted between the two antagonists. The conflict rapidly reached its climax, and by the end of 1949, the Communists had won the struggle on the China mainland, while the Nationalists had taken refuge on Formosa.

Clearly, many of the most important causes of the Nationalists' defeat during this decisive period were military ones. The Nationalists pursued a self-defeating strategy; instead of undertaking offensives aimed at seeking out and destroying the main mobile and guerrilla units of the Communists, they holed up for the most part in isolated, vulnerable, defensive positions, allowing the Communists to concentrate their forces, to besiege, attack, and overwhelm such positions one by one. Moreover, the Nationalists made many disastrous errors in specific military operations. For example, Generalissimo Chiang decided, against the best military advice available, to commit some of the Nationalists' most modern forces and equipment to Manchuria at a time when Communist forces there controlled much of the countryside and supply and communication lines linking Manchuria to the rest of the country were highly vulnerable. Perhaps most important of all, however, was the deterioration of morale among the Nationalists' troops. Many crucial battles during 1947–

49 were lost without a fight, as hundreds of thousands of Nationalist troops simply defected or surrendered.

. . . Although the Nationalist forces clearly had the upper hand in mid-1946 — possessing much greater supplies of modern military equipment and, according to American official estimates, outnumbering the Communists' forces by roughly three million to one million — the Communists seized the strategic initiative during 1947, carrying the struggle from Manchuria into north China; during 1948, the military balance shifted decisively in favor of the Communists; and by 1949, the Communists had achieved basic military control over the China mainland. Communist victories, in rapid succession, at Tsinan, Mukden, and Hsuchow in late 1948, and at Tientsin and Peking in early 1949, followed by the crossing of the Yangtze and the capture of Nanking and Shanghai in the spring, sealed the Nationalists' fate on the China mainland. Everything thereafter — in the northwest, southwest, and south — proved to be simple mopping-up operations for the Communists.

The underlying causes of the Nationalists' collapse can hardly be sought by analyzing these military events alone, however. Actually, the demoralization and defeat of the Nationalist forces were merely a reflection of the much broader and more basic process of political, economic, and social disintegration that took place in Nationalist-held China during 1946–49 at a headlong pace. . . .

As mentioned earlier, most of these forces of disintegration had first begun to be felt some years previously, during the Sino-Japanese War. After they had appeared, it was clear that the Nationalist regime would need to undergo a heroic political regeneration in order to survive. But once full-scale civil war had broken out, instead of the situation improving, the Nationalist regime collapsed with calamitous speed.

It is difficult to assess the relative importance of the varied factors causing this disintegration. The political disunity existing within Nationalist China was certainly one of the most fundamental. Many areas of so-called Nationalist territory — some of them ruled by old-style warlords — became increasingly alienated from the Central Government; eventually, several of these areas came to terms separately with the Communists, and even those that tried to resist could not do so on their own with any success. Within the Nationalist Party itself, clique politics and factionalism reached a point where unified, vigorous action — either to solve the problems in Nationalist-held territory or to fight against the Communists — was virtually impossible. Runaway inflation reached incredible proportions, creating great instability and insecurity, ensuring corruption, crippling government finance, and causing general demoralization. China's intellectuals, who have played an extremely important role in modern Chinese history and have affected the political climate far more than their real political power would seem to warrant, became almost universally disaffected, drifting steadily toward the Left. They were not alone in their disaffection. Other key groups were almost equally estranged. Many of China's businessmen, for example, lost all faith in the government, and reached the point where they, too, actively hoped for a change of regime — even a Communist takeover. Organized labor, while playing almost no significant insurrectionary role of the sort once expected by orthodox Marxists, nevertheless became increasingly dissident when the deterioration of economic conditions resulted in general hardship. In the countryside, conditions stagnated, and the peasants were subjected to an enormous and growing economic burden. There was no general uprising of the peasants in Nationalist-held territory, but neither was there any significant positive support of the existing regime. Even the most politically passive peasants were predisposed to react favorably when the Communists, backed by their revolutionary armies, suddenly appeared and promised them "liberation" and land. In short, public morale throughout Nationalist China reached such a low point that the basis for any effective resistance to the Communists completely disappeared.

The actual pattern of Communist takeover in China hardly fitted into traditional Marxist concepts, however. It was not an urban insurrection, a *coup d'état*, or even, for that matter, a general peasant revolt. Instead, the pattern was one of systematic military conquest — or, in the latter stages, of negotiated surrenders imposed by the Communists, who by then had achieved clear military predominance. True, the Communists had built their revolutionary armies in certain areas of rural China by arousing and organizing peasant revolts, but then these armies moved rapidly and efficiently to seize and occupy the rest of the country during the climactic civil-war years of 1946–49.

The relative ease of the final Communist takeover was a result in part, of course, of the strength of the Chinese Communist revolutionary movement forged during the previous two decades of armed struggle, but the speed of the takeover was also the result of the completeness of the demoralization, disintegration, and collapse of the Nationalist regime on the mainland.

THE CIVIL WAR, 1945–1949

Defeat by Military Default

F. F. LIU

F. F. Liu, a former combat and staff officer in the Kuomintang army, gives in this scholarly study of the military history of modern China a careful analysis of the factors contributing to the military weakness of his government. Among the various causes are two on which he lays special stress: the inefficient command structure of the Kuomintang army and Chiang Kai-shek's political reliance on the Whampoa officers because of their indubitable loyalty. Liu also points to the Kuomintang dilemma in Manchuria: the acquisition of that territory he regards to be militarily perilous but politically necessary. The excerpt below begins with the formation by the Chinese Communist Party of the People's Liberation Army in July 1946, immediately following the Chang-chun-Szepingkai campaign of March-June and the imposition by "the Americans" of a truce in Manchuria on June 6th.

THE nationalists, more from fear of losing American support than as a reflection of Chinese national sentiment, went along with the United States attempt to negotiate a Kuomintang-Communist coalition. The communists had no intention of incorporating their armies in the national forces and in July 1946 boldly announced from Yenan the creation of a "people's liberation army," formed from the amalgamation of the Eighth Route Army, the New Fourth Army, and the newly formed Red forces in Manchuria. They were to prove a far more difficult foe than the Japanese had been. The nationalists had long feared that such would be the case.[1]

The communists in Manchuria clashed with the Kuomintang forces at Szepingkai and, facing a capable strategist like General Pai Chung-hsi, who fled to Manchuria to direct the over-all operation, saved themselves from destruction only by a rapid retreat across the Sungari River into Harbin, a city under the shadow of Soviet military power across the border. . . . Then, on the sixth of June 1946, the Americans imposed a truce in Manchuria, and this intervention permitted the communists a breathing spell in which to recover and consolidate.

While the "truce" lasted the communists prepared for future tests of Mao Tse-tung's policy, which stressed the concentration of overwhelmingly superior forces designed to meet fractions of the enemy's hosts and to dispose of them one by one. The political strategy which accompanied this plan featured movements toward greater unity between the officers and men within the communist ranks, the improvement and extension of public relations with the masses of the people, techniques to demoralize the enemy, and elaborate programs

[1] Even during the Sino-Japanese war the nationalists had a premonition of this, and the people were saying, "The Japanese are only lice on the body of China, but communism is a disease of the heart."

F. F. Liu, *A Military History of Modern China, 1924–1949* (Princeton: Princeton University Press, 1956), pp. 243–45, 253–60, 264–67, 270. Reprinted by permission.

for the indoctrination and conversion of prisoners of war.

The government forces initially envisioned a large-scale, all-out campaign against the Reds, but soon modified their plans to stress concentrated offensives in Shangtung and northern Shensi, the two spearheads of the communist front. The sheer inertia of a war-weary populace and the rapid deterioration of military morale contributed to the ever-decreasing momentum of the nationalist effort. Meanwhile, behind the scenes, competent generals like Li Tsung-jen,[2] Pai Chung-hsi, and Hsueh Yueh were being given a fast shuffle by the Whampoa clique, which, considering that it had won the war, was engaged in dividing the spoils. The much-needed unity of command waned and there was an increasing reluctance on the part of various commanders to render that unswerving loyalty which the leaders could no longer compel.

By 1947 the government's military leadership was in incredible confusion, and the rate of turnover in the important field commands soared to a new high. Famous fighting generals like Sun Lien-chung, Hsueh Yueh, and Wu Chi-wei were relieved of their commands. The capable military strategist General Pai Chung-hsi was pigeonholed in an office without power, while the chief of the supreme staff was removed to Mukden and the commanding general of the new First Army relegated to a post of secondary importance. The ministry of defense and the supreme staff were disrupted, there was no continuity in the field commands, and everywhere there was uncertainty, confusion, and stalemate. Many of the generals who were not from the Central Army took the reshuffling as evidence of distrust and discrimination and were even further alienated from the Whampoa group.

[2] Li Tsung-jen of the Kwangsi faction was elected Vice-President in April 1948, against the wishes of Chiang Kai-shek. He was Acting President during the period of Chiang's "withdrawal" from the Presidency from January 1949, to March 1950. [Editor's note.]

With no sure hand on the helm, the entire Nationalist Army was rendered incapable of aggressive and coordinated offensives against the communists. Dissatisfaction at the top filtered down to the lowest levels of the troops. Those commanders who were not sure of themselves kept their troops behind city walls or, if compelled to venture forth, dug in elaborately at every halt on the march, tiring the men unnecessarily and giving rise to a hesitant, indecisive defensive psychology highly harmful to their fighting morale. Foremost among the many causes of indecisiveness was Generalissimo Chiang's policy of conserving the strength of his direct units rather than employing them in aggressive operations against the communists.

In wartime an army not constantly put under the test of battle is bound to lose its offensive spirit, and with it, the war. Prolonged garrison duties and the absence of a rotation plan caused the average soldier to despair of ever being discharged. Meanwhile, life in the army went on in a country where inflation had so devaluated the soldier's low pay that his salary would hardly permit him to feed himself adequately. In the less disciplined units the soldiers wrung an occasional decent meal out of the farmers by force, by such action losing popular support for their government which, although constantly claiming to be winning battles, had in effect begun to lose the war.

The communists, on the other hand, were assiduous in their efforts to maintain good relations with the populace. They avoided some of the problems of inflation by issuing food and small luxuries directly to the troops rather than paying them in cash. At the same time the communists were able to aggravate the government's economic plight by cutting lines of communication and preventing foodstuffs from reaching urban areas, thus sending city prices higher and forcing the government to pay ruinous prices to maintain troops in the cities.

Continuity in command structure was another strength of the Reds. Battle-tested generals were placed at the highest levels without favoritism, and merit won promotions for deserving junior officers. From top to bottom, the communist forces were well indoctrinated with the party's political and military objectives and unified by party loyalties.

In mid-1946 the government troops, some 3,000,000 men, outnumbered the communists almost three to one. Demobilization cut government forces to 2,600,000 by the end of the same year, while the communist forces grew. There was considerable evidence that substantial portions of the demobilized nationalists, as well as the disbanded Manchukuo and other puppet armies, were absorbed by the communist forces. As civil war became inevitable, the government resorted to conscription and, by late 1947, had built its strength back up to 2,700,000 men. The hope to train 200,000 of these men by the end of 1948 in American-aided military training centers, however, was not fulfilled. Throughout 1948 the nationalists maintained an estimated strength of 2,730,000 men, but by February of the next year heavy losses had reduced their strength to 1,500,000 — a reduction of 45 per cent of the government's total troop strength in a mere four and a half months. The National Government's official estimate of the relative strengths was as follows:

	SEPTEMBER 1945		JUNE 1948	
	Government Forces	Communist Forces	Government Forces	Communist Forces
Men	3,700,000	320,000	2,180,000	2,600,000
Rifles	1,600,000	160,000	980,000	970,000
Artillery	6,000	600	2,100	2,280

The communist statistics on the same account are:

	Government Forces	Communist Forces	Ratio
July 1946	4,300,000	1,200,000	3.58:1
June 1947	3,730,000	1,950,000	1.9:1
June 1948	3,650,000	2,800,000	1.3:1
June 1949	1,490,000	4,000,000	0.3:1

With the strength of the communist armies steadily on the increase, the government was now committed more and more to positional warfare, and it became overextended and, for reasons of prestige, debarred from withdrawal or consolidation. . . .

Of all the critical decisions of the postwar period, none seem to be of greater historical significance than the National Government's resolve to reoccupy Manchuria. Although such overextension of its forces was perilous militarily, politically the government had no alternative but to commit itself to the arduous task of reasserting its sovereignty over an area for which China had fought her long war against Japan. She could not long remain passive while the communists seized that territory, despite the rights granted to the Soviet Union in the Yalta Agreement and despite the fact that the Russians were firmly entrenched in Manchuria. Soviet sympathy for the Chinese Reds prompted them to deny to the nationalists the use of port facilities, thereby making expeditious entry into Manchuria impossible and giving the communists time to organize in the area, to consolidate their local control, and to equip a military force with former Japanese weapons.

China was determined to reoccupy Manchuria even though General Wedemeyer hastened to point out the dangers of such an occupation in view of the logistical difficulties of supporting operations there while at the same time controlling China proper. In Washington, General Eisenhower viewed the nationalist effort as a gross overextension of forces. But Chinese political considerations outweighed military logic.

The communists in Manchuria had grown into no mean force. Early in 1947, employing their strategy of "offensive defence," they were strong enough to present a considerable threat. For the first time in the history of Chinese communist warfare, the Reds had graduated from guerrilla tactics to the use of tanks and artillery. Their first offensive was deftly turned back by government forces under General Sun Li-jen,[3] but soon afterwards Sun was relieved of his command and assigned to direct a training program at Nanking. His departure gave freer reign to the incompetence of his superior, General Tu Yü-ming, one of the most influential of Whampoa's generals and field commander of northeast China. There was little cooperation between him and his superior, General Hsiung Shih-hui, director of the generalissimo's headquarters in Manchuria. It was common knowledge that the Whampoa I-ch'i (the graduates of that military academy's first class) were so arrogant that they considered themselves obliged to deal independently with the generalissimo himself and not answerable for cooperation to their fellow generals. Two such were Tu and Hsiung, and the lines of responsibility in the command structure became unclear and the leadership confused.

Following their unsuccessful first offensive, which Sun had stopped, the communists unleashed three successive drives, wearing down the government defenders of the key cities. The communist strategy was aimed at forcing the government troops to disperse their forces and then decimating them through successive counter-blows. By the autumn of 1947 the situation had become so urgent that the government recalled Hsiung Shih-hui and replaced him as Manchurian commander with the capable Ch'en Ch'eng.[4] Ch'en's immediate purge of the army not only disposed of a number of corrupt officers but unfortunately, in the disbanding of large numbers of ex-Manchukuo troops, also sent over to the communist side many disgruntled men whom the government could ill afford to lose. . . .

The fifth communist offensive, in May 1947, which covered most of Manchuria,

began to show the communist superiority in artillery power as well as in the number and technical proficiency of their troops: an indication that the communist training program had reaped results. The communist forces surrounded the government forces in Kirin, Changchun, and Szepingkai. Almost an entire government army was cut off from the rest of China, and the problems of maintaining some 700,000 government personnel (of which only about 250,000 men were effective combat troops) became almost insurmountable. The lines of communication from China proper were long and tenuous, and the communists effectively eradicated them. It became a question of fight or starve. . . .

. . . The winter brought a communist offensive in 40° sub-zero weather which resulted in the capture of a number of the government's fortified strongholds. The defeats forced the replacement of Ch'en Ch'eng by General Wei Li-huang as commander in Manchuria. To supply the 150,000 to 200,000 troops in the immediate Mukden sector, the government resorted to a costly airlift, but the combined capacity of civilian and military air transports could barely deliver a third of the enormous tonnage requirements. In terms of financial drain, in September 1948, General Ho Ying-ch'in, then defense minister, reported to a secret session of the Legislative Yuan that the whole allotment of the military budget for the latter half of 1948 had been completely spent on air-supplying a single city, Changchun, for two months and four days.

At the height of the crisis two of the most vital military posts — chief of the supreme staff and commander of the ground forces — were conferred upon men of no conspicuous abilities. The new appointees, Generals Ku Chu-t'ung and Yü Han-mou, were stanch supporters of the generalissimo. That is all that could be said for them.

In central and eastern China, the key cities of Kaifeng and Tsinan fell in July and September 1948, respectively. The generalissimo ordered his forces to fight to the

[3] Sun Li-jen is a graduate of Virginia Military Institute and is considered by many as "one of the best-educated and most battle-experienced younger generals." [Editor's note.]
[4] Now Vice-President of the Republic of China in Taiwan. [Editor's note.]

last to hold the two walled fortresses, but defeatism was growing among the troops and many defected to the communist attackers. The loss of these two points convinced the generalissimo at last that the old strategy of holding key points or strongholds at all costs would have to go, and that a reexamination of nationalist errors in strategy, tactics, training, and organization of field units would have to be made. By then, however, it was too late.

Considering the confusion at planning levels it was surprising that even greater errors in strategy had not been committed. There was no efficient leadership to integrate plans, to implement them, and to direct their execution. The supreme general staff — the nerve center of the armed forces — had been hastily patched up after the 1946 reorganization and had failed to become a strategic directorate. It was simply a tactical command organ. The armed forces operated on a "six months' plan"! The confusion prompted the generalissimo himself to take over certain phases of the direction of military operations, which merely added to the chaos by having certain operational orders issued directly without the knowledge of the supreme staff and the minister of defense. He personally conducted regular operational briefings in the map room of his residence, issuing directives for field operations which were often transmitted directly to the combat units in the forms of *shou-ch'i* (personal instruction) or *shih-ts'an* (directives from the president's personal military staff). Usually only a few persons participated, including his personal chief of staff, the deputy chief of supreme staff, and the director of G-3. The defense minister was not always invited for the conference. If the briefing was held at 9 P.M., Chiang's personal directive would perhaps reach the front-line unit concerned by the next morning — already impractical for execution (although it had to be obeyed under threat of punishment) since the fast-moving communist force would be many miles away after a

night of forced marching. In one such case three conflicting orders (from the generalissimo, the chief of the supreme staff, and his immediate superior) were given to the commander of an army group who was just about to administer the *coup de grâce* to an encircled enemy. Under threat of severe punitive action he was forced to abandon his attack and to relieve some other government forces of no importance to the entire military outcome and, worse still, the besieging communist force had already left the scene by the time his force rushed to the designated spot!

In October 1948, during the crucial stage of the Manchurian campaign, Generalissimo Chiang himself went to Peiping, whence he directed the entire operation alone without reference to the minister of defense or to the supreme staff to which he had previously promised to delegate all power of military command and administration. But Chiang's earlier interference had muddled the command structure and now, despite the basic soundness of his order for simultaneous attacks from Mukden and Changchun in order to effectuate the breakout of government force from Changchun, his commands were not obeyed in full. General Wei Li-huang's force did not lash out from Mukden in full strength. In despair, one of the garrison units, the 60th Army (Yunnanese), revolted and turned its guns on the loyal New Seventh Army. The latter, a partly American-trained force, was the backbone of the city's defense forces. On the twentieth of the month Changchun and its starving defenders fell into communist hands.

Not only was there bungling in the command in Manchuria, but the general strategy was also all wrong. The government ought to have capitalized upon its indisputable advantages: greater mobility along the seacoast and control of the air. As it was, the Chinese air force played but a small part even during the most critical of the battles in Manchuria. It came into prominence only after the humiliating fall of Mukden[5] — bombing the communists who had occupied the city from such altitude that the operation was considered a complete waste. It is incredible that interservice cooperation could have been so slight, especially since the air forces at the time were being commanded by an army general.

The loss of Manchuria and some 300,000 of its best troops spelled the beginning of the end for the nationalists. Nearly 360,000 communist troops from Manchuria were now free to move against China proper.

With the nation in turmoil and all China north of the Yangtze in communist control, the generalissimo yielded to pressures from within and without the government and announced his decision to retire. He left Nanking for Fenghua, his birthplace and a beautiful coastal town in the province of Chekiang, on January 22, 1949. In accordance with Article 49 of the Chinese constitution, Vice-president Li Tsung-jen assumed the acting presidency.

Meanwhile Generalissimo Chiang prepared to make Taiwan (Formosa) a fortified redoubt against the communists. To the island fortress went almost the entire government gold reserve, much of the equipment shipped from the United States, and large concentrations of trusted troops, the navy, and the air force. Though outwardly cooperating with the acting president, the generalissimo was in effect maintaining independent political and military authority. Li had no unified control of nationalist China. An able general, Li did not even control the larger portion of the army. The generalissimo's power continued to be felt in military affairs. What Li needed — the money, the troops, the naval and air support, unity of command — all was denied him. The largest single force that the acting president could rely on were the 350,000 troops under General Pai

Chung-hsi, whose headquarters in central China command was at Hankow. Altogether the government had at that time about 1,800,000 regular army troops; of these Chiang still maintained firm control of two major army groupings under the command of T'ang En-po and Hu Tsung-nan. . . .

At midnight on April 20, 1949, the communists crossed the Yangtze at several strategic points, with their main concentrations at Kiangyin and south Anhwei. General Tai Yung-kwan, the bribed commander of the key Yangtze fortress at Kiangyin, protected the communist crossing and shelled the nationalist naval units. Another one-time aide of Chiang, Commodore Lin Tsun, went over to the communist side with his naval squadron at Nanking. The remaining naval and air forces failed to provide effective support for the defending forces on shore. By the secret order of General T'ang En-po, the Central Army units which had been assigned to resist any communist crossing into the lower Yangtze area were *withdrawn*. They were reassigned to defend the city of Shanghai by the secret order of the generalissimo in retirement. The battle was lost, first of all, because of no unity in command.

At the eleventh hour Chiang and Li had a serious difference over the grand strategy. The heart of the matter lay in Li's desire to mobilize and concentrate all available forces to hold China south of the Yangtze, his belief that the provinces of Kwangtung and Kwangsi and the southwest should be regarded as the stronghold from which there would be no retreat. Chiang, while ostensibly concurring in principle, was basically unwilling to commit his forces to a last-ditch stand on the mainland. Formosa was, in his view, to be the refuge and the last bastion of nationalist arms.

. . . History will eventually provide the answer to the question and indicate whether Chiang's policy of the Formosan bastion or Li's policy of a concerted stand in south China was the better strategy. Meanwhile, the Red banners of commu-

---

[5] Mukden was taken by Communist forces on November 4, 1948. [Editor's note.]

nism have been hoisted all over the mainland of China.

In eleven months the communist banners of Mao Tse-tung and Chu Teh had advanced 2,000 miles from Mukden to Chengtu, averaging well over six miles a day. Theirs was a fine fighting force, but historians must nevertheless conclude that in the communist conquest of the vast mainland of China much of their success must be attributed to the default of the Chinese nationalist military power — a great military force taxed by eight years of supreme effort against Imperial Japan and betrayed from within by corruption, maladministration, and dissension in high places.

Victory by Psychological Warfare

MICHAEL LINDSAY

Michael Lindsay, Lord Lindsay of Birker (1909–), has taught economics, and international relations in China, England, Australia, and the U. S. Press Attaché at the British Embassy in Chungking in 1940, he is better known for his extended wartime experience with the Communist 18th Group Army in 1942–45, which has given him an unusual background for assessing the military factors in the Chinese civil war as they relate to the Communist forces. In this article, written at a time when the Kuomintang exuded great confidence in its own military power, Lindsay predicts instead of a Kuomintang success the early victory, barring unforeseen changes in the balance of power, of the Communist army owing to its mobile organization, effective guerrilla tactics, the party's popular land program, and widespread support in the countryside. Moreover, he underscores the decisive importance of Communist psychological warfare in swaying the allegiance of the Kuomintang troops and in causing them, to borrow Lenin's words in the Russian revolutionary context, to vote with their feet. If Professor Lindsay's estimate of four or five years needed for the Communist victory turned out to be somewhat conservative, it may be noted that the conservativeness of his estimate was even shared by Mao Tse-tung, who, until the Huai Hai Campaign of November 1948, had similarly predicted victory by mid-1951.

THE striking thing about the civil war in China is the difference between the armies on either side. The Kuomintang has a regular army of over two million, some with American training and many with American equipment. It also has an American-trained air force. The Communists have a regular army of only about one million. They have no air force; and much of the army is still equipped with what it was able to capture from the enemy or make in primitive local arsenals. It is hard to say just how much Japanese material the Communists took over in Manchuria, but it was certainly not enough to re-equip more than a part of their army.

So far the Kuomintang has succeeded in taking every major objective, and it might seem that if Chiang Kai-shek decided to fight an all-out civil war he could

Michael Lindsay, "Who Will Win the Civil War in China?" *Virginia Quarterly Review*, XXIII, No. 2 (March, 1947), pp. 193–94, 202–08. Reprinted by permission of the author and publisher.

certainly win it. Some Kuomintang generals talk of complete victory in less than six months. What this leaves out of account is the fact that the Communist army has always been fighting a much better equipped enemy and has done it very effectively.

The Communist position now is far stronger than it was in 1928, when Chu Te started with ten thousand men and only two thousand rifles for them. But it took the Kuomintang till 1934 to drive Chu Te out of South China. The Communist position is also stronger than it was in 1938 against the Japanese, and the Japanese never managed to eliminate the Communist armies. In fact, after 1943 the Communists were gaining. By 1945 the Japanese controlled less of North China than they had in 1940 at the start of their biggest anti-Communist campaigns.

In many ways the military situation in North China now is similar to that in 1938. The Communists hold most of the countryside and face a better equipped enemy holding the railways and major cities. They hold a great deal more than in 1938 when they had almost nothing in Manchuria and only small forces in Shantung. The Communist army is also larger and rather better equipped than it was then. However, the situation is sufficiently similar for the experience of the war with Japan to be used in predicting what is likely to happen now.

If Chiang Kai-shek could keep up military pressure against the Communist areas on the same scale as the maximum Japanese efforts, he might get a final military decision. But he would find it hard to do this without continued foreign support and it would, at any rate, take years rather than months. If the Communists could inflict sufficiently heavy losses on the Kuomintang armies and if they could force their dispersal by spreading guerrilla warfare into other parts of China, then they would have a good chance of final victory.

For both sides the only chance of a fairly quick victory depends on psychological rather than military warfare. If Chiang Kai-shek could win popular support in the countryside away from the Communists, their situation would quickly become hopeless. Equally, if the Communists could produce large scale desertions from the Kuomintang armies, they might win quite quickly. In the earlier civil war Chiang Kaishek said that the problem of exterminating the Communists was seventy per cent political and only thirty per cent military. This is just as true today.

The Kuomintang armies are larger than were the Japanese forces. . . . However, they are not necessarily stronger. . . . Throughout the war the Japanese could defeat Kuomintang armies greatly superior in numbers. Japanese organization was better and the quality of Japanese officers was always far higher than that of the Kuomintang. . . .

There is also the important question of morale. Probably few Kuomintang troops are as unreliable as some of the locally recruited puppets but, equally, none are as resistant to psychological warfare as the Japanese. Throughout the war only a few hundred individual Japanese deserted to the Communists; but one complete Kuomintang army went over in October, 1945, and two complete divisions in the summer of 1946.

The main factor in Kuomintang successes is that so far the fighting has been the kind for which the Kuomintang army is specially suited and for which the Communists have neither the equipment nor the experience and training. The Kuomintang army has always had the tradition of fighting regular positional warfare and, even against the Japanese, it tended to despise guerrilla methods.

So long as the better units with American equipment remain intact, the Kuomintang will be able to win positional battles. Like the Japanese, it will be able to take any particular objective if it is prepared to pay the price, though it will probably have to take much higher losses than the Japanese ever did.

Within six months or perhaps a year the Kuomintang should be able to establish control of all the railways and major cities and probably to capture Yenan[1] and important points off the railways. But this would be only the beginning of the war. The Communists would try to make the Kuomintang advance as expensive as possible and to keep their own armies intact.

Once the Communists decided to fight an all-out civil war, their obvious strategy would be to spread guerrilla warfare. It should not be too difficult for them to rebuild their organization in the old New Fourth Army areas of Central China. Then, too, in the last few years there have been peasant revolts in Kuomintang provinces in South and West China. A continuance of the draft and of war-time taxation would make fresh revolts likely. If the Communists could get a few organizers and a small supply of arms into these areas, they could build up new guerrilla bases. Even small-scale activity of this kind would tie up large numbers of the Kuomintang army.

The critical phase of the war would come when the Kuomintang tried to eliminate the Communist armies and get control of the countryside. This attempt would have to be made. Until the Kuomintang armies can be demobilized, there is no possibility of balancing the budget and stopping inflation. While the Communists hold a good deal of the country, normal trade will be impossible, and economic chaos is much worse for the Kuomintang-held cities than for the Communist-held countryside, which consists of almost self-sufficient village communities.

The fighting would then be of the type which favors the Communists. The Kuomintang would have to start to rebuild the Japanese fort and blockade-line system and to raid the Communist bases. In this kind of fighting their losses would be extremely heavy.

Another important factor is that it would become impossible to isolate the army from Communist propaganda. The Kuomintang armies have been recruited by a very unfair and corrupt draft system, and in many units the men are badly fed and badly treated. Most Kuomintang armies have been kept together by rather terroristic discipline and have tended to disintegrate once they were scattered by a defeat. It would be extremely difficult to maintain morale when the army was scattered in small garrisons. Even if Kuomintang garrisons did not actually desert, they might easily become useless. Like many of the puppet garrisons without Japanese stiffening, they might reach an understanding with the Communist forces. . . .

After a year or so of this kind of fighting, the Kuomintang might lose the war. Many of their best troops would have been lost. Much of the army would be demoralized. What remained would have to be more and more widely dispersed to prevent the spread of guerrilla warfare. The Communist armies, fighting their own type of warfare, would have lost far fewer men and might have captured considerable equipment.

Once the Kuomintang failed in their attempt to control the countryside, their collapse might be quite rapid. Their economic position would deteriorate, and as soon as the Communists seemed to be winning, there would be a rush to get on the winning side. Few armies in China except the well-established Communist units have enough political training to feel strongly about changing sides. Some commanders have already made a complete circle. Wang Tao in Shantung started as a Kuomintang guerrilla leader, joined the Japanese when they seemed to be winning, went over to the Communists towards the end of the war, and recently went back to the Kuomintang.

In a straight fight between the two sides in China, this would be the most probable course of the war. It is hard to say just how long it would be before the final Kuomintang collapse, but the Communists would have a fair chance of winning in four or five years.

---

[1] Yenan was taken by Kuomintang troops in March 1947. [Editor's note.]

With large-scale American assistance the Kuomintang would have a better chance. New equipment and expert instructors would be available to keep their armies up to full strength. Large foreign loans and economic assistance would lessen the burden of the war and prevent economic collapse. American troops defending important cities and rail lines would free Kuomintang armies for attack. Most important, continued American intervention would have a very great effect on morale. The Kuomintang would feel that they were fighting with an indefinitely large reserve of military supplies and economic assistance behind them.

With enough American assistance the Kuomintang might be strong enough to restore all the Japanese fort system and extend it still further. Here again success would be cumulative after a certain point. Loss of territory would compel the Communists to reduce their army. When the situation began to appear hopeless, the army might start to disintegrate and the civilian population to feel that it was useless to make further sacrifices to resist Kuomintang control. The Communists might be reduced to a few small groups in the wilder mountain areas, as they were in South China or Manchuria after 1934. Judging from the earlier civil war or the fighting with the Japanese, this also would take a minimum of four or five years, even with all-out American assistance to the Kuomintang. It might take much longer.

In either case the prospect for China is gloomy if the two parties simply fight it out. The war would go on for years and would be very destructive. . . .

For psychological warfare which offers the only chance of a quick end to the war, the Communists are in much the stronger position. In North China Chiang Kai-shek will find it hard to live down his use of the Japanese and his taking over of the puppet armies. These were the only forces he could use to oppose the Communists immediately after V-J Day, but he can hardly win popular support in areas where he is still represented by troops which served under the Japanese. The puppet armies did not massacre the civilian population on the same scale as the Japanese, but they were quite as bad in looting and raping.

In the long run Chiang Kai-shek can only win popular support by providing better government than the Communists, and here he faces a dilemma. He cannot win a civil war unless he provides good government and he cannot provide good government if he wants to fight a civil war. The only group in the country which can be relied on in a civil war is the old ruling class of officials and landlords. But they are reliable only because they stand to lose by the sort of reforms that the Communists have carried out. The people who would be willing to carry out reforms stand for very much the same sort of program as the Communists. If they were in power, there would be very little to fight about and both sides would probably be willing to reach a peaceful settlement.

It is only a slight exaggeration to say that everything the Communists have done can be found in Kuomintang programs or in unenforced Kuomintang laws. Sun Yat-sen's program forty years ago called for "the equitable redistribution of land," and the Communist agrarian policy since 1937 has been based on laws which the Kuomintang government passed in 1930. The real issue is the form of local government. The Communists have been able to put through their reforms because they have been willing to arm the people, and in China possession of a gun is nine points of the law. As long as the local officials and landlords controlled the gendarmerie and Peace Preservation Corps, they could nullify any change they disliked. When the people in the village with arms were the village militia, there was no one in the village who could stop the village council from enforcing reforms.

On paper Chiang Kai-shek is prepared to outbid the Communists. He offers rent restriction to one third of the crop instead of three eighths under the Communists. However, he is determined to put back authoritarian local government and this puts power in the hands of people who have always nullified reforms.

The Communists are in a much stronger position. There is no doubt about their ability to attract the peasantry because they offer the ordinary farmer what he wants: that is, a larger share of what he produces and a better political and social status. Even in the old South China Soviets, where the organization was much less efficient and much more terroristic than in the present North China Areas, the Communists had strong peasant support. If they can restrain their extremists, who might like to go back to the old land-redistribution policy,[2] they may even retain some support from landlord and business groups. . . .

The main Communist handicap in win-

[2] The Land Law of the Soviet Republic in Kiangsi, promulgated on November 7, 1931. [Editor's note.]

ning support from more educated groups is suspicion of Russian influence. In fact, the Russian connection has been very slight, and both the theory and the practice of the Chinese Communists have diverged very widely from those of the Russian and other Western Communist Parties. However, they have always followed the Russian line on foreign policy and lost much support by failing to denounce the Russian looting of Manchuria.

If the Communists were prepared to make a definite repudiation of Russia, they could probably get general support from the intelligentsia and might win over many Kuomintang officers. This could give them a quick victory in psychological warfare. Even with the handicap of suspected Russian influence they have a strong enough appeal on their internal record and program to have a good chance of winning the support of the majority of the population throughout China and of the lower ranks of the Kuomintang armies.

Popular Discontent and Creeping Paralysis

JOHN LEIGHTON STUART

John Leighton Stuart (1876–1962), born in China of Presbyterian missionary parents, was himself an ordained minister after completing his high school and college education in the U. S. Founder of Yenching University in 1919, he was also its president at the time of his appointment as American Ambassador in July 1946 on the recommendation of General George C. Marshall. Though not known as a forceful diplomat, he remained on good terms with both Chiang Kai-shek and the Communist negotiator Chou En-lai, the cordial relations being doubtless facilitated by the presence of Yenching graduates in both parties. Stuart left China and retired from public life soon after Mao Tse-tung declared in July 1949 the lean-to-one-side policy of the Chinese Communist Party. He subsequently attributed the failure of his ambassadorial mission in part to America's China policy of coalition government and in part to his government's lack of practical knowledge of China and its people.

As for the failure of the Kuomintang, he stated in the selection below that it was due principally to a "misunderstanding" the public had of the motives of the Generalissimo and, by extension, of the Kuomintang in the brief space of time following V-J Day. This adverse turn of events, owing to the combination of economic, military, and psychological deterioration and accentuated by Communist agitation and a widespread feeling of war-weariness, marred the public image of Chiang Kai-shek and seriously undermined public confidence in the government. To illustrate his view, he pointed to the attitudes and actions of the students, the most sensitized sector of Chinese society that he knew so well.

I HAD reached Shanghai from America about the end of April, 1946, and was detained there for various reasons for about two weeks, anxious to return to the Yenching campus where many problems were awaiting me. But Philip Fugh[1] who had flown to Shanghai to meet me urged that I ought to stop off in Nanking to pay my respects to the Generalissimo. . . .

The visit with Chiang Kai-shek was well worth the inconveniences involved. My last one had been in Chungking the previous September, and it was pleasant to see him settled again in the capital. In the course of our talk, he asked me my impressions of the situation, and I replied that they were much worse than what I had gathered from American press reports. He then asked what suggestions I had and, after thinking a moment, I told him I would like to sum these up in one that went to the heart of the issue. This was that he should himself lead in a new revolutionary movement for internal reforms with something of the adventurous enthusiasm with which he had originally joined the Kuomintang under Sun Yat-sen when this was really dangerous and that I felt he could thus again rally the students and younger intellectuals now so discontented but eager for a leader whom they could wholeheartedly follow. With them as volunteer propagandists he could win back the waning public confidence and be again the symbol of the national will, as he undoubtedly had been during the Japanese war. This was the only way to overcome the Communist menace, but, in doing so, he would

[1] Stuart's confidant and private secretary. [Editor's note.]

also be carrying into effect the third of "The Three Principles," the People's Livelihood. He nodded assent, but as I was to learn later it was one thing to secure this, and quite another to stir his will to resolute action.

The government continued to pass reform measures which were but rarely carried out. But it was too much weakened in material resources and too depressed in spirit to do much more than keep going. The combination of economic, military and psychological deterioration was causing a creeping paralysis. The patient was too ill to recover without the administration of a strong tonic. If nothing succeeds like success, nothing fails like failure. Public confidence in the government was waning steadily, and this mood was permeating its own officials of all ranks. Student strikes and demonstrations, many of them Communist instigated, became more frequent and these, as always, were symptoms of swelling discontent. Anti-American feeling was deepening, due chiefly to the belief that we were delaying the Communist party's overthrow of a rotten government. This was revealed in the violent student agitations over any minor incident that would otherwise pass unnoticed.

In China, even more perhaps than elsewhere, the students serve as an excellent barometer of popular trends. They are the most highly sensitized element. Their reactions are more intelligent and spontaneous, and they have fewer inhibitions. Chinese students are as a class passionately patriotic. Their good motives can be cleverly utilized for political purposes. With the rapidly spiraling inflation and the increased cost of living there was all through

From *Fifty Years in China*, by John Leighton Stuart. Copyright 1954 by John Leighton Stuart. Reprinted by permission of Random House, Inc., pp. 162–63, 188–89, 192–95, 275–77.

1947 and 1948 growing student unrest due latterly to economic as well as political causes. Food riots dramatized this. During the Japanese war the government had wisely subsidized students in exile colleges in the far interior. Even so, their hardships and discomforts were acute, but they willingly endured these. The practise of subsidies for food and for almost everything else continued after V-J Day in the government institutions. But as the food became scarcer and less palatable they found fault with a government which could not give them peace and better living conditions. Fighting against Communists, who were also Chinese after all, failed to arouse the same patriotic loyalty as when the enemies were Japanese. Student sympathy was also more with radical, socialistic movements than with a government which most of them regarded as hopelessly reactionary. Dejection, even despair, was prevalent among all student groups. It was not only that the food was bad. Clothing, warmth, textbooks, laboratory equipment, the quality of classroom instruction, employment after graduation — everything in short that touched their lives was as wrong as the food. . . .

Even with students, therefore, mere bodily existence bulked larger in their thinking than national problems or ideological arguments. In September, 1947, it was estimated that in Tsinghua and Yenching Universities[2] about ninety to ninety-five percent did not want China to become communized. But a year later, this figure had dropped to sixty to seventy percent. They felt so disconsolate that they believed that even Communist domination could not be worse. It would at any rate bring peace and a better livelihood. To those who were not responding to the appeal of communism, what would happen if the National Government collapsed did not matter. They were not looking that far ahead.

During the year 1948 the Chinese Government achieved two really notable reforms which partially disproved the charges that it could not help itself.

One was the meeting of the new National Assembly, postponed from the previous December, and the presidential elections. There were irregularities in the election of delegates and controversies over their status. In the Assembly itself there were disorderly shoutings and many crudities. None the less, the first step had been taken in representative government by popular election and in public exposure of the attendant abuses. There was real freedom of debate including open criticism of the government. The actual balloting for President and Vice-President was carried through with meticulous care and literally glaring publicity under powerful searchlights. There could not have been any violations and apparently none were attempted. As always, the Generalissimo's personality was the dominant feature, but there was conscious restraint on his part as he tried to discipline himself to observe constitutional procedure. . . .

The other reform was in currency. Inflation was reaching fantastic figures. The volume and weight of paper money required even for minor transactions was burdensome. Everyone was trying to get rid of it before it became completely valueless, and speculation was rife as to when and how this point would be reached. Obviously something had to be done. The government leaders studied the problem and on August 19, 1948, issued a new currency known as the "Gold Yuan" to be pegged at four to one United States dollar, to be guaranteed by actual government assets, and to be kept within the amount of these with the assistance of a committee of competent and highly respected Shanghai citizens who would publish a monthly statement of accounts. There would be rigid price and exchange control. One Gold Yuan was estimated at 3,000,000 of the old *fapi* dollars. Patriotic citizens were urged to exchange their gold or silver holdings for the new notes. Strict regulations were an-

[2] Neighboring universities just outside of Peiping. [Editor's note.]

nounced governing export, import and other trading activities. The whole scheme had been kept secret, which alone was a notable achievement in China. The Premier[3] had confided it to me a few days before, and I was greatly pleased. As I pointed out to him and others the scheme would only succeed if rigidly enforced, if it won popular support, and if military victories could recover the lost confidence of the people in their government. He acknowledged that this was their last chance. If it failed, they had in mind no other conceivable device.

For the first month or so the plan went well. The government had shown vision, courage and determination. The monetary measures, while not wholly satisfactory, were perhaps about as effective as could have been designed. The people of moderate means responded nobly and the government soon collected over $200,000,000 from this source, although the really wealthy were conspicuous by their avoidance of the opportunity. . . .

Slowly at first, then more rapidly, things began to go wrong. . . . Inexorable economic laws were already making themselves felt in the exchange rate and rising commodity prices, and . . . military debacle sent these spiralling into a new inflation. This would have come sooner or later in any case, for when the government income was less than fifteen percent of its expenditures, it could not have been otherwise. The economic hardships of the populace became more acute, especially those of the salaried classes. The discontent sank deeper and was more openly expressed.

This may be an appropriate place for me to give my final estimate of Chiang Kai-shek. During the six months of my association with the Marshall mission, the Generalissimo was always the dominant figure. It was he who made all decisions for the government or party, and it was he who was most feared or denounced by the Com-

munist delegates. It was always interesting to watch how quickly he understood what was being said to him, how incisively he grasped its essence, and how tenaciously he held to that first reaction. He is a man of strong will power and indomitable courage. But as so often happens his failings are due to the excess of his best qualities. Any judgment of him should be formed against the background of his cultural heritage and of the precarious circumstances amid which he has carried his terrific responsibilities. With this in mind, and by comparison not only with the history of Oriental despotism but also with contemporary dictators, Chiang Kai-shek deserves credit for the restraint with which he has generally acted.

I never had any question as to the moral character of the Generalissimo despite some of the political measures he took which might seem wrong according to our contemporary European and American standards. I am convinced that he has faithfully acted for what he believed to be the best interests of his country. It has not always been easy for him to distinguish between his personal and his country's advantages. But in contrast with the venality, avarice, indolence and cowardice of many of the traditional "Mandarins," his nobility of character stands out as exceptional.

When Chiang Kai-shek burst into prominence after the death of Sun Yat-sen, he was a popular hero. The new movement under its youthful leader had vigor and high idealism. But as he successfully pursued his efforts to unify the nation the shadow of the Japanese policy of continental expansion grew darker. Chiang seemed to be doing nothing effectual about it. Was he in sympathy with the Japanese militarists? Was he so much preoccupied with the nascent Communist uprising that he failed to sense the imminent Japanese threat? No, he knew that there must first be political and military preparedness. He had the sense to exercise restraint in order to avoid inviting — and possibly warranting — a Japanese attack.

The Japanese invasion of north China in

[3] Chang Ch'ün, President of the Executive Yuan. [Editor's note.]

the summer of 1937 was undoubtedly hastened by the increasing unity and strength of the National Government under Chiang's progressive planning. During the following eight years of incredible devastation and suffering for almost the entire population, of defeat and withdrawal ever further inland, he was the inspiring embodiment of the popular will. It was the essence of democracy because he ruled not by political organization, nor by military power, but by the united support of all classes of the people, to all of whom he was the symbol of their own will to resist the invader at any cost. Despite many sordid or stupid happenings in the conduct of the war, the Chinese people rose to a sublime height in their patient endurance and unflinching resistance. All this would have been ineffective, however, without the right leader.

In striking contrast with this almost universal esteem, was the steadily increasing opposition to the Generalissimo after V-J Day when his popularity was at its zenith. After three years of civil war he lost in large measure the confidence of his people. This curious phenomenon compels an attempt at explanation. First, the Kuomintang had genuinely aimed at erecting a democratic government of the western type, yet except for a limited number of idealists the actual dynamic was nationalism. The Generalissimo was anxious to effect these reforms, but while he was engrossed in pressing military or administrative problems, the ancient evils reasserted their hold. The system was not sufficiently rectified. A second factor was the steadily mounting inflation and consequent economic distress. When resisting Japan, this was loyally accepted, but in what seemed to be senseless and inconclusive civil strife, discontent festered and deepened and was inflamed by clever Communist propaganda and infiltration. Not a few dissident political leaders and military commanders were actually plotting against the Generalissimo; some were in collusion with the Communists, all of them augmenting the turmoil and the defection from Chiang. Another contributing cause to Chiang's waning popularity was that, because of the suppression of Communist infiltration, the methods he adopted gave the impression to the people of what seemed to be his high-handed violation of civil rights. From his own standpoint he was fighting against an enemy utterly unscrupulous in its methods. The only practicable defense, to him, was resort to emergency measures. He recognized the real nature of the Chinese Communists before almost any others of his fellow countrymen or of Americans or other "foreigners" living in China, and he resolutely decided to risk misunderstanding, unpopularity and even defeat in following out his own better comprehension of this crucial issue.

WORLD WAR II: TURNING POINT TOWARD DEFEAT

Body Blow of War

EDWIN O. REISCHAUER

Professor Reischauer (1910–   ) served in the State and War Departments during World War II, and was a special assistant to the director of the Office of Far Eastern Affairs, Department of State, in 1945–46. At the time of his appointment as Ambassador to Japan in 1961, he was Professor of Far Eastern Languages at Harvard University and Director of the Harvard-Yenching Institute. In this selection he attributes the Kuomintang debacle to the effects of the Second World War and to larger historical ("natural") forces that conditioned the broad pattern of political developments in China.

THERE were probably two major reasons for the Kuomintang failure. An obvious one was Japanese aggression against China. The Japanese, moved in part by fear of what might happen if China did become fully united and strong, started in 1931 a limited war in which they seized Manchuria, the economically most promising part of China, and destroyed part of the city of Shanghai. Then after slower and somewhat more disguised encroachments in north China, they started what was meant to be a second limited war in 1937. But this time the Chinese refused to accept limited losses from a limited war. The fighting continued, and the Japanese kept seizing more and more of China in an effort to force the Chinese to capitulate. Chiang was driven out of all his principal industrial cities and chief areas of agricultural production and was forced back into the mountains of western and southern China. The economy of China was shattered and the Kuomintang regime completely disrupted. These protracted and devastating wars forced on the Chinese by Japan are in themselves certainly ample explanation of the failure of Chiang's regime to accomplish its aims.

There was, however, perhaps another and more fundamental reason for the failure of the Kuomintang. This was the very magnitude of the task it faced and the difficulty for any one group to achieve the whole of it. To the extent that the Kuomintang succeeded, it created a confirmed and privileged leadership that looked on further changes with growing mistrust and distaste. As the years went by, the Kuomintang increasingly came to represent the *status quo* and thus began itself to stand in the way of progress. This natural process seems to have been much accelerated by the wars with Japan, which forced the Kuomintang to rely on groups not in sympathy with its original objectives and to make many compromises of principle that might otherwise have been avoided. Under these conditions the natural slowing down of the Kuomintang movement turned into an open rout in the early postwar years, as corruption and inefficiency undermined the government from within and made it incapable of coping with mounting economic chaos.

In any case, whatever may have been the basic reasons for Kuomintang failure, there can be no doubt that Chiang's regime began to appear in Chinese eyes to be, not the wave of the future, but a wave of the past that was starting to recede. Increasing numbers of younger nationalistic Chinese gave up hope that the Kuomintang would build a strong China capable of winning equality with the West and started to cast about for some new way of achieving this goal, just as their elders had done two or three decades earlier. The disenchantment started with the intellectual classes, which had for long been attracted by Communist ideology, but it spread rapidly to other groups during the latter part of the war and the early postwar years.

War and Inflation

CHANG KIA-NGAU

Years of service in banking and communications in the Kuomintang government have afforded Chang Kia-ngau (Chang Chia-ao, 1888–), brother of Carsun Chang, a unique qualification to interpret the economic problems behind the inflation which embattled and engulfed Kuomintang China. From the outbreak of the Second World War in 1937 to the Kuomintang debacle in 1949, the government, he says, failed to seize three strategic moments — in 1938–39, 1941, and 1945 — to launch much-needed fiscal reforms. Instead of facing difficult economic tasks with resolve and courage, the Kuomintang government committed serious errors in policy and management, and relied with disastrous consequences on excessive deficit financing and note-issuing. It is Mr. Chang's view that the only effective way to avert "a vicious spiral of inflation" is to halt the process of inflation "at the earliest possible stage," a view he regards to be "axiomatic." The fate of the Kuomintang government was sealed, he concludes, when the political leadership in both the budget and the banking system, acting with scant regard for the economic health of the nation and understanding little of the principles of economics, placed "prestige and outward military power" above sound judgment.

SHORTLY after the end of the war the government returned to the coastal region, there to base its power on the more developed urban sector of the economy. The traditionally coastal and urban-minded government authorities relished their return to the more modern and more abundant port cities, abandoning the interior with the new urban sector it had created, and the vast rural resources as if they were of no importance. Partly because of successful Communist efforts to frustrate the government's restoration of communications between the North and South, attempts to integrate the economies of the two regions failed.

Chang Kia-ngau, *The Inflationary Spiral: The Experience in China, 1939–1950* (Cambridge: The Technology Press of Massachusetts Institute of Technology; and New York: John Wiley & Sons, Inc., 1958), pp. 99–103, 364–67. Reprinted by permission of the Massachusetts Institute of Technology.

As it developed, for a short period the urban sector became almost self-sufficient, with a basic orientation toward world markets. . . . In this setting, the government embarked upon a new program of releasing inflationary pressures with little initial thought about restraining their effect on price levels. In the fragmented conditions of the economy, these inflationary pressures came to be released almost entirely within the coastal, urban sector, a condition which in turn placed great strain upon the balance of payments since foreign trade became the major avenue by which total supply within the sector could be increased. As it finally developed, the behavior of prices in the coastal sector came to be associated with the state of foreign supply and with abundance (or lack) of foreign exchange.

As time progressed, inflationary responses between the two major domestic sectors grew farther and farther apart. This can be seen from the striking contrast between the high level of prices in the coastal urban markets, and the low level of prices in the interior. The price indexes for September 1947 (the last month for which the wholesale price indexes of major cities were published by the government) gave a clear picture, as shown in Table 27.

TABLE 27. WHOLESALE PRICE INDEX, SEPTEMBER 1947 [1]

(Jan.—June 1937 = 100)

Coastal Cities	Index	Interior Cities	Index
Shanghai	4,635,700	Chungking	2,590,240
Tientsin	4,574,905	Changsha	3,481,400
Tsingtao	6,304,000	Lanchow	3,636,300
Canton	4,169,327	Kunming	2,444,775
Foochow	4,529,710	Kweiyang	1,564,323

[1] Source: Based on statistics compiled by Directorate-General of Budgets, Accounts and Statistics.

So far as anti-inflationary policy was concerned, this meant that overt price control measures were destined to fail unless the supply situation could be improved either by the integration of the economy into a working whole or by the provision of almost unlimited access to foreign exchange. Since little was done in regard to the former, anti-inflationary policy in this period became primarily a matter of foreign trade and foreign exchange control. . . .

Meanwhile, government spending rapidly increased the money supply, and inflationary pressures continued to grow. The government's part in this process is shown in Table 28.

TABLE 28. POSTWAR INFLATIONARY PRESSURES GENERATED BY THE GOVERNMENT

Year	Increase of Government Expenditures	Increase of the Deficit	Increase of the Note Issue
1946	3.2 times	4.2 times	3.6 times
1947	5.7 times	6.2 times	8.9 times
1948[1]	30.0 times	30.0 times	22.4 times

[1] The rate of increase of expenditures and of the deficit in 1948 is based on figures published for the first half of that year.

The government also failed to take account of the inherent pressure of the purchasing power accumulated during the war years. This force was now being brought into play in the coastal sector, where it was hoped supplies would be plentiful. Thus supply and demand were already badly out of balance, and the addition of the new money could only produce the most inflationary of the alternative responses. . . . Supplies of goods were increasingly withheld from the market in anticipation of further price rises; consumers became increasingly unwilling to accumulate monetary savings. Both factors tended to accentuate the velocity of the turnover of money. Sellers had little real opportunity to replenish inventories which had been drawn down by years of wartime demands; and the movement of prices fostered reluctance on the part of merchants to make available what little inventories they had for sale.

All these phenomena first became evident in a few major cities, eventually spreading throughout the urban sector. Inflationary pressures finally seeped through to the entire rural sector, but with varying degrees of intensity according to local conditions of supply and demand. Farmers in the hinterland realized that the decline of the value of the currency was irreversible, and that they would fare better by hoarding their products or by exchanging them for consumer goods. Thus the urban sector was subjected to a new double pressure: the decreasing inflow of foodstuffs and other agricultural raw materials from the commercialized hinterland, and the increasing demand for consumer goods. The lack of foodstuffs brought with it rising prices and wages, and the shortage of raw materials for light industry entailed higher prices for consumer goods turned out by such industry.

Having failed to control prices by measures affecting the dynamics of the domestic economy, the government now had to depend for its price control on the effects of foodstuff and raw materials imports. It attempted to distribute these either at an unrealistically low exchange rate or at controlled prices. This approach is most clearly seen in control of cotton imports after 1946 and rice during 1947 and 1948. The imported food was used mainly to help meet the requirements of the population of some eleven million in the five eastern cities of Shanghai, Tientsin, Peking, Nanking, and Canton, while the cotton imports were to supply about 80 per cent of the cotton industry located in the coastal urban sector.

Although low-priced food and cotton imports somewhat relieved the supply shortage in the urban sector, they also put a damper on prices of domestic production of these commodities. This increased the farmers' preference for hoarding their production, even in the agricultural areas adjacent to the coast, and further aggravated the supply problem in the urban sector. Moreover, the continued excess of imports over exports exhausted China's dwindling reserves of foreign exchange. This eventually forced curtailment of raw material and capital goods imports needed by domestic industries. The net result was the failure of domestic industrial production to restore prewar levels of output.

In this manner the input-output relationships in the urban sector were disorganized, and the flow of goods between the cities and the hinterland also came to a virtual standstill. The economy on which Nationalist power was based became squeezed between monetary expansion on one side and the contraction of the supply of agricultural and industrial products on the other.

Retrospection suggests the conclusion that the government both overestimated the ability of the urban sector to absorb the large additional supplies of money and underestimated the strength and contribution which the rural sector might have made toward the survival of Nationalist China. As it turned out, inflationary pressures could not be smoothly transmitted from the city to the farm, there to be equalized and relieved; instead, they created additional barriers to economic intercourse between the sectors.

It is axiomatic that, once a vicious spiral of inflation has set in, it becomes increasingly difficult to halt the process. Attempts should have been made to curb Chinese inflation at the earliest possible stage. However, since tax increases and other measures calling for greater sacrifice required strong and broad political support, we concede that the Chinese government may have wished to choose the most favorable and strategic moments to launch sweeping reforms. One such opportunity presented itself in late 1938 and early 1939, when the government was forced to fall back upon the undeveloped hinterland and when the population was heart and soul behind the leadership's announced decision to prosecute a long war for national survival. A second opportunity occurred at the end of 1941, when the entry of the United States into the Pacific war seemed to make final victory for the first time a virtual certainty and provided the much needed psychological lift and financial support to make a determined effort to set the country's finances in order once for all. A third strategic occasion was to present itself at the end of World War II when it should have been apparent to the government that reconstruction could not proceed without monetary stabilization through basic reform and when the call for reform would have united all true patriots. Yet time and again the government failed to launch a program of basic fiscal reform until it was no longer feasible to do so.

To a large extent the government's inability to raise revenue by non-inflationary means and to absorb surplus demand through savings and taxation was due to its fear of losing popular support, of offending vested interests, and of facing a difficult task with courage and determination. Not possessing the wisdom and courage to undertake unpopular measures, the government could of course have reduced the scale of its spending. But it persisted in its refusal to take any effective step to trim expenditure and, overemphasizing the importance of prestige and outward military power, it underwrote political and military expenditures regardless of their economic consequences. It was curiously blind to the fact that in the long run economic health is a prerequisite of political power. It sought an easy way out of its financial difficulties, only to court eventual disaster.

Given the inflationary pressures which its policy failures helped to generate, the government then sought to suppress the symptom of inflation by price control and to increase production by further expansion of credit. Thus the momentum of inflation was given further impetus while the increase of prices refused to respond to the application of political pressure. In fact, direct controls could not be effectively enforced because the government lacked the means of enforcement, namely, an efficient and incorruptible administrative apparatus technically equipped to carry out its detailed assignments with skill, fairness, and loyalty. Yet because of its failure to institute basic financial reforms, the government was increasingly compelled to resort to direct and discretionary controls of credit.

production, prices and wages, and foreign trade and exchange, success in which was particularly unlikely in view of the absence of the requisites. In short, it came to concentrate its efforts on the *symptoms* of inflation rather than on its *causes*.

When the government had to admit failure in all its economic measures, it once again resorted to political means. It came to stake its political future and prestige on an abortive currency "reform," only to find that its political influence was no longer adequate, that popular confidence had been dissipated through the years, and that it was merely hastening the final debacle.

Chinese inflation also taught the lesson that executive domination of both the budget and the banking system may prove to be a most unwholesome combination. Where the government budget is left in the hands of the political leadership instead of being closely scrutinized by a properly constituted authority, and the central bank is treated as the government's disbursing agent, the ability to create money may become a curse instead of a boon to the economy. In China arbitrary control of the budget and the central bank were vested in the political leadership. This leadership, failing to understand the nature of the economic forces with which it dealt, chose to ignore them. The government could find no alternative with which to finance itself. Inflation was to run its course, and the ultimate fate of the government was sealed. Economic instability finally led to a general loss of confidence in the Nationalist government, and total collapse of political and social morals followed. Into this chaos and political and moral vacuum almost any militant group promising a clean sweep could have moved without strong opposition; and the Communists were there to take full advantage of the situation.

The Enthronement of Reaction

JOHN S. SERVICE

Born in China in 1909 of missionary parents, John S. Service was appointed Foreign Service Officer by the U. S. Department of State in 1933, when he returned to China following the completion of his education at Oberlin College. His official duties in Asia brought him to various parts of China, to Tokyo on the staff of SCAP, and to Calcutta, but the most important assignment, as events of later years would have it, was that in 1943–45, when he was on loan to the staff of the Commanding General of the China-Burma-India theater. As political officer to General Joseph W. Stilwell and later to General Albert C. Wedemeyer, "his job was to get every bit of information that he possibly could . . . as to what was going on in China." It was during this period that he wrote the reports that were to figure prominently in the loyalty investigations in the fifties.

The report below, written on June 20, 1944, and reaffirmed by Service in 1950 before a Senate investigating committee as a correct reflection of existing conditions in China, is his most extensive analysis of the weaknesses of the Kuomintang government. He observed that the Kuomintang had not only ceased to be the unifying and progressive force in China, but was also "incapable of averting a debacle by its own initiative." He further said that Chiang Kai-shek, conservative and megalomaniacal, had lost his sense of political touch, and that the Kuomintang, selfish and reactionary, had become a power-hungry group. China's hope, he concluded, lay in the formation of a "broadly based democratic government" of all liberal elements within the country.

B. *The position of the Kuomintang and the generalissimo is weaker than it has been for the past 10 years.*

China faces economic collapse. This is causing disintegration of the army and the government's administrative apparatus. It is one of the chief causes of growing political unrest. The generalissimo is losing the support of a China which, by unity in the face of violent aggression, found a new and unexpected strength during the first 2 years of the war with Japan. Internal weaknesses are becoming accentuated and there is taking place a reversal of the process of unification.

1. Morale is low and discouragement widespread. There is general feeling of hopelessness.

2. The authority of the Central Government is weakening in the areas away from the larger cities, and government mandates and measures of control cannot be enforced and remain ineffective. It is becoming difficult for the government to collect enough food for its huge army and bureaucracy.

3. The governmental and military structure is being permeated and demoralized from top to bottom by corruption, unprecedented in scale and openness.

4. The intellectual and salaried classes, who have suffered the most heavily from inflation, are in danger of liquidation. The

John S. Service, "The Situation in China and Suggestions Regarding American Policy," June 20, 1944, reproduced in U. S. Senate Committee on Foreign Relations, *Hearings on State Department Employee Loyalty Investigation*, 81st Congress, 2nd session, 1950, pp. 2036–42.

academic groups suffer not only the attrition and demoralization of economic stress, the weight of years of political control and repression is robbing them of the intellectual vigor and leadership they once had.

5. Peasant resentment of the abuses of conscription, tax collection, and other arbitrary impositions has been widespread and is growing. The danger is ever-increasing that past sporadic outbreaks of banditry and agrarian unrest may increase in scale and find political motivation.

6. The provincial groups are making common cause with one another and with other dissident groups, and are actively consolidating their positions. Their continuing strength in the face of the growing weakness of the Central Government is forcing new measures of political appeasement in their favor.

7. Unrest within the Kuomintang armies is increasing, as shown in one important instance by the "young generals conspiracy" late in 1943. On a higher plane the war zone commanders are building up their own spheres of influence and are thus creating a "new warlordism."

8. The break between the Kuomintang and the Communists not only shows no signs of being closed, but grows more critical with the passage of time; the inevitability of civil war is now generally accepted.

9. The Kuomintang is losing the respect and support of the people by its selfish policies and its refusal to heed progressive criticism. It seems unable to revivify itself with fresh blood, and its unchanging leadership shows a growing ossification and loss of a sense of reality. To combat the dissensions and cliquism within the party, which grow more rather than less acute, the leadership is turning toward the reactionary and unpopular Chen brothers clique.[1]

10. The generalissimo shows a similar loss of realistic flexibility and a hardening of narrowly conservative views. His growing megalomania and his unfortunate attempts to be "sage" as well as leader — shown, for instance, by "China's Destiny" and his book on economics[2] — have forfeited the respect of many intellectuals, who enjoy in China a position of unique influence. Criticism of his dictatorship is becoming more outspoken.

These symptoms of deterioration and internal stress have been increased by the defeat in Honan and will be further accelerated if, as seems likely, the Japanese succeed in partially or wholly depriving the Central Government of East China south of the Yangtze.[3]

In the face of the grave crisis with which it is confronted, the Kuomintang is ceasing to be the unifying and progressive force in Chinese security, the role in which it made its greatest contribution to modern China.

C. *The Kuomintang is not only proving itself incapable of averting a debacle by its own initiative; on the contrary, its policies are precipitating the crisis.*

Some war-weariness in China must be expected. But the policies of the Kuomintang under the impact of hyperinflation and to the presence of obvious signs of internal and external weakness must be described as bankrupt. . . .

1. *On the internal political front the desire of the Kuomintang leaders to perpetuate their own power overrides all other considerations.*

The result is the enthronement of reaction.

The Kuomintang continues to ignore the great political drive within the country for democratic reform. The writings of the generalissimo and the party press show that they have no real understanding of that term. Constitutionalism remains an empty promise for which the only "preparation" is a half-hearted attempt to establish an unpopular and undemocratic system of local self-government based on collective responsibility and given odium by Japanese utili-

---

[1] The C. C. Clique of Ch'en Kuo-fu and Ch'en Li-fu. [Editor's note.]

[2] *Chinese Economic Theory.* [Editor's note.]
[3] The Japanese forces began in May, 1944, the fateful South China drive toward the Kweilin air base. [Editor's note.]

zation in Manchuria and other areas under their control.

Questions basic to the future of democracy such as the form of the Constitution and the composition and election of the National Congress remain the dictation of the Kuomintang. There is no progress toward the fundamental conditions of freedom of expression and recognition of non-Kuomintang groups. Even the educational and political advantages of giving power and democratic character to the existing but impotent People's Political Council are ignored.

On the contrary, the trend is still in the other direction. Through such means as compulsory political training for government posts, emphasis on the political nature of the army, thought control, and increasing identification of the party and government, the Kuomintang intensifies its drive for "Ein Volk, Ein Reich, Ein Fuhrer" — even though such a policy in China is inevitably doomed to failure.

The Kuomintang shows no [intention of] relaxing the authoritarian controls on which its present power depends. Far from discarding or reducing the paraphernalia of a police state — the multiple and [omnipresent] secret police organizations, the gendarmerie, and so forth — it continues to strengthen them as its last resort for internal security. (For the reenforcement of the most important of these German inspired and Gestapo-like organizations we must, unfortunately, bear some responsibility.)

Obsessed by the growing and potential threat of the Communists, who it fears may attract the popular support its own nature makes impossible, the Kuomintang, despite the pretext — to meet foreign and Chinese criticism — of conducting negotiations with the Communists, continues to adhere to policies and plans which can only result in civil war. In so doing it shows itself blind to the facts: that its internal political and military situation is so weak that success without outside assistance is most problematic; that such a civil war would hasten the process of disintegration and the spread of chaos; that it would prevent the prosecution of any effective war against Japan; and that the only parties to benefit would be Japan immediately and Russia eventually. Preparations for this civil war include an alliance with the present Chinese puppets which augur ill for future unity and democracy.

2. *On the economic front the Kuomintang is unwilling to take any effective steps to check inflation which would injure the landlord capitalist class.*

It is directly responsible for the increase of official corruption, which is one of the main obstacles to any rational attempt to ameliorate the financial situation. It does nothing to stop large scale profiteering, hoarding, and speculation — all of which are carried on by people either powerful in the party or with intimate political connections.

It fails to carry out effective mobilization of resources. Such measures of wartime control as it has promulgated have remained a dead letter or have intensified the problems they were supposedly designed to remedy — as for instance ill-advised and poorly executed attempts at price regulations.

It passively allows both industrial and the more important handicraft production to run down, as they of course must when it is more profitable for speculators to hold raw materials than to have them go through the normal productive process.

It fails to carry out rationing except in a very limited way, or to regulate the manufacture and trade in luxury goods, many of which come from areas under Japanese control. It shows little concern that these imports are largely paid for with strategic commodities of value to the enemy.

It fails to make an effective attempt to reduce the budgetary deficit and increases revenue by tapping such resources as excess profits and incomes of landlords and merchants. It allows its tax-collecting apparatus to bog down in corruption and inefficiency to the point that possibly not more than one-third of revenues collected reach the government. It continues to spend huge government funds on an idle and useless party bureaucracy.

At best, it passively watches inflation gather momentum without even attempting palliative measures available to it, such as the aggressive sale of gold and foreign currency.

It refuses to attack the fundamental economic problems of China such as the growing concentration of landholdings, extortionate rents and ruinous interest rates, and the impact of inflation.

D. *These apparently suicidal policies of the Kuomintang have their roots in the composition and nature of the party.*

In view of the above it becomes pertinent to ask *why* the Kuomintang has lost its power of leadership; *why* it neither wishes actively to wage war against Japan itself nor to cooperate wholeheartedly with the American Army in China; and *why* it has ceased to be capable of unifying the country.

The answer to all these questions is to be found in the present composition and nature of the party. Politically, a classical and definitive American description becomes ever more true: the Kuomintang is a congerie of conservative political cliques interested primarily in the preservation of their own power against all outsiders and in jockeying for position among themselves. Economically, the Kuomintang rests on the narrow base of the rural gentry landlords, the militarists, the higher ranks of the government bureaucracy, and merchant bankers having intimate connections with the government bureaucrats. This base has actually contracted during the war. The Kuomintang no longer commands, as it once did, the unequivocal support of China's industrialists, who as a group have been much weakened economically, and hence politically, by the Japanese seizure of the coastal cities.

The relation of this description of the Kuomintang to the questions propounded above is clear.

The Kuomintang has lost its leadership because it has lost touch with and is no longer representative of a nation which, through the practical experience of the war, is becoming both more politically conscious and more aware of the party's selfish shortcomings.

It cannot fight an effective war because this [is] impossible without greater reliance upon and support by the people. There must be a release of the national energy such as occurred during the early period of the war. Under present conditions, this can be brought about only by reform of the party and greater political democracy. What form this democracy takes is not as important as the genuine adoption of a democratic philosophy and attitude; the threat of foreign invasion is no longer enough to stimulate the Chinese people and only real reform can now regain their enthusiasm. But the growth of democracy, though basic to China's continuing war effort, would, to the mind of the Kuomintang's present leaders, imperil the foundations of the party's power because it would mean that the conservative cliques would have to give up their closely guarded monopoly. Rather than do this, they prefer to see the war remain in its present state of passive inertia. They are thus sacrificing China's national interests to their own selfish ends.

The Kuomintang cannot unify the country because it derives its support from the economically most conservative groups, who wish the retention of China's economically and socially backward agrarian society. These groups are incapable of bringing about China's industrialization, although they pay this objective elaborate lip service. They are also committed to the maintenance of an order which by its very nature fosters particularism and resists modern centralization. Countless examples can be given to show the line-up of the party with the groups that oppose modernization and industrialization — such as connections with Szechwan warlords and militarists. The Kuomintang sees no objection to maintaining the economic interests of some of its component groups in occupied China or in preserving trade with occupied China, the criterion of which is not the national interest but its profitability to the engaging groups. This explains why free China's imports from occupied China consist largely of luxuries, against exports of food and strategic raw materials. It is therefore not surprising that there are many links, both political and economic, between the Kuomintang and the puppet regime.

E. *The present policies of the Kuomintang seem certain of failure; if that failure results in a collapse of China, it will have consequences disastrous both to our immediate military plans and our long-term interests in the Far East.*

The foregoing analysis has shown that the Kuomintang, under its present leadership, has neither the ability nor desire to undertake a program which could energize the war and check the process of internal disintegration. Its preoccupation with the maintenance and consolidation of its power must result, to the contrary, in acceleration rather than retardation of the rate of this disintegration. Unless it widens its base and changes its character, it must be expected to continue its present policies. It will not of its own volition take steps to bring about this broadening and reform. The opposite will be the case: Precisely because it has lost popular support, it is redoubling its efforts to maintain and monopolize control.

F. *There are, however, active and constructive forces in China opposed to the present trends of the Kuomintang leadership which, if given a chance, might avert the threatened collapse.*

These groups, all increasingly dissatisfied with the government and the party responsible for it, include the patriotic younger army officers; the small merchants; large sections of the lower ranks of the government bureaucracy; most of the foreign-returned students; the intelligentsia, including professors, students, and the professional classes; the liberal elements of the

Kuomintang, who make up a sizable minority under the leadership of such men as Sun Fo,[4] the minor parties and groups, some of which like the National Salvationists enjoy great prestige; the Chinese Communist Party; and the inarticulate but increasingly restless rural population.

The collective numbers and influence of these groups could be tremendous. A Kuomintang official recently admitted that resentment against the present Kuomintang government is so widespread that if there were free, universal elections 80 percent of the votes might be cast against it. But most of these groups are nebulous and unorganized, feeling — like the farmers — perhaps only a blind dislike of conditions as they are. They represent different classes and varying political beliefs — where they have any at all. They are tending, however, to draw together in the consciousness of their common interest in the change of the *status quo.* This awakening and fusion is, of course, opposed by the Kuomintang with every means at its disposal.

The hopeful sign is that all of these groups are agreed that the basic problem in China today is political reform toward democracy. This point requires emphasis. It is only through political reform that the restoration of the will to fight, the unification of the country, the elimination of provincial warlordism, the solution of the Communist problem, the institution of economic policies which can avoid collapse, and the emergence of a government actually supported by the people can be achieved. *Democratic reform is the crux of all important Chinese problems, military, economic, and political.*

It is clear beyond doubt that China's hope for internal peace and effective unity — certainly in the immediate future . . . and probably in the long term as well — lies neither with the present Kuomintang nor with the Communists, but in a democratic combination of the liberal elements

[4] Sun Fo was President of the Legislative Yuan, 1932–48 and President of the Executive Yuan, 1948–49. [Editor's note.]

within the country, including these within the Kuomintang, and the probably large sections of the Communists who would be willing, by their own statements and past actions, to collaborate in the resurrection of a united front.

Given the known interest and attitudes of the Chinese people, we can be sure that measures to accomplish the solution of these problems will be undertaken in earnest by a broadly based government. Such a government — and only such a government — will galvanize China out of its military inertia by restoring national morale through such means as the reduction of the evils of conscription and stopping the maltreatment and starvation of the troops. Such a government — and only such a government — will automatically end the paralyzing internal dissension and political unrest. Such a government — and only such a government — will undertake the economic measures necessary to increase production, establish effective price controls, mobilize national resources, and end corruption, hoarding, speculation and profiteering.

It is of course, unrealistic to assume that such a broadly based democratic government can be established at one stroke, or that it can immediately achieve the accomplishment of these broad objectives. But progress will be made as, only as, the government moves toward democracy.

STRUCTURAL AND PROGRAMMATIC WEAKNESSES OF THE KUOMINTANG GOVERNMENT, 1928–1949

Contradictions between Program and Practice

TANG TSOU

Professor Tsou, Associate Professor of Political Science at the University of Chicago and Research Associate at the Center for the Study of American Foreign and Military Policy, is especially recognized for his scholarly study on Sino-American relations during the decade of the forties. In the following excerpts, he sees the seeds of the Kuomintang debacle in the party's failure to realize the Principles of Nationalism, Democracy, and People's Livelihood, a failure further compounded by the "fatal" effect of the Second World War and by the Generalissimo's "mystic" tendency to regard himself as the very embodiment of the Chinese nation.

From the date of its establishment in Nanking in April, 1927, the Nationalist government suffered from a series of basic contradictions between its program and its practice. Dr. Sun Yat-sen advocated a policy of "land to the tiller," and in 1926 the Nationalist party adopted a program of restricting rent to 37.5 per cent of the annual total produce of the land. But the Nationalist government consistently failed to put its program into effect. The failure to reform land tenure, to reduce interest rates, and to curb usury [alienated] the peasant. In the theory and program of the Nationalist party, political tutelage by one party was a temporary device to educate and prepare the people for the task of building a constitutional democracy. But the actual trend of the Nationalist government was toward intrenchment of the dictatorship of the party and the concentration of power in the hands of one man. The determination of the Nationalist party to give overwhelming power to the executive and little to the popular assembly in successive revised drafts of the constitution, the rise of such semisecret organizations as the "Blue Shirts," and the imitation of the trappings of Fascist countries disillusioned the Western-educated and Western-oriented liberals. One of the driving forces behind the movement toward a personal dictatorship was the desire for a strong and effective government. Yet Chiang Kai-shek never succeeded in building a united party and an efficient government.

The Nationalist party rose to power on a wave of anti-imperialism among the Chinese people. Its popular support was generated in the first place by its nationalistic program. But, in the years after the Japanese invasion of Manchuria, it consistently

Tang Tsou, *America's Failure in China, 1941–1950* (Chicago: The University of Chicago Press, 1963), pp. 48–49, 122–23. Reprinted by permission.

refused to face the grave challenge posed by Japan to China's territorial integrity and national existence. The government's timidity and vacillation in the face of Japanese aggression stood in sharp contrast to the savage civil war against the Communists, whatever may be said for its policy of "internal pacification before resistance to external attack." As Japan quickly consolidated her control over Manchuria and Jehol and progressively infiltrated Inner Mongolia and North China, the support of the educated class for the Nationalist party began to be dissipated.

Prior to 1937 there were some positive accomplishments. Thirty relatively modern army divisions and a modern air force were created. There were improvements and reforms in the technical fields of administration, finance, and communication. The greatest achievement, however, was the steady extension of the authority of the central government over semi-independent military and political leaders in the various outlying provinces. A semblance of unity had been achieved by the astute use of force and stratagem where feasible and by political compromise when necessary. If Japan had not attacked in 1937, the Nationalist government might have continued to consolidate its power and authority by the sheer weight of its military strength and financial resources. Such a government, though far from popular, might have survived for a substantial period because of the weakness of the opposing forces.

The Sino-Japanese War dealt the Nationalist government crushing blows, which eventually proved fatal. In the first place, it decimated the Nationalist army and drove the Nationalist government from its home base, causing a new surge of the centrifugal tendency in Chinese politics. Secondly, it gave the Communists opportunity to expand their control over the most important regions of China. Third, it greatly weakened the upper classes, which had been the strong and capable supporters of the Nationalist government, and created conditions which alienated the middle classes from the government. Finally, the stresses of war caused a demoralization of the bureaucracy and the army.

. . . The Generalissimo was confirmed in his belief that the United States was so dependent on him to protect her Far Eastern interests and so lacking in firmness of purpose in the pursuit of her policy that she would finally yield to his insistent demands and accept his views, no matter what he did or refused to do. Thus, he was emboldened in his endeavors to push as far as possible what he considered to be the interests of his government and his party. This proved to be a fatal miscalculation and was to become one of the causes of his downfall.

The basic source of this error was the Generalissimo's inability to find and promote the common interests between himself and others or, in other words, his narrow conception of his, his government's, and China's interests. His habit of pushing his interests as far as possible and exacting every ounce of advantage in any situation rendered it difficult for others to work with him. His unbounded confidence in his political and military judgment, his faith in his infallibility, and his mystic sense of identity with the nation made him arrogant and unsusceptible to advice and argument.

Internationally, his attitudes and policies alienated the United States, which alone could have given him the needed support. Within China, they precluded the possibility of building up a regime broadly based on the divergent social and political groups in China, while the Chinese Communists, in spite of an original ideology prescribing a monopoly of power by one social group, confronted him with a policy of developing the "progressive forces," winning over the "middle-of-the-road" forces, and isolating the "die-hards." Thus, the seeds of his downfall were imbedded in the amazing political skill which had given him his earlier successes.

Chiang Kai-shek and Kuomintang Dictatorship

CARSUN CHANG

Carsun Chang or Chang Chün-mai (1886–   ), a noted third party leader and a brother of Chang Kia-ngau, studied law and political science in Japan and Germany, as did many young progressives of his time. While in Germany in 1919–22, he reached the enduring conviction, as did few Chinese reformers, that the Anglo-Saxon tradition of government was "the best and safest model for China." After the Kuomintang established the Nanking Government in 1927, Chang published a magazine called the *New Way*, through which he opposed political tutelage as "nothing less than totalitarianism," and because of which he was compelled to leave China. Upon his return in 1931, he became the founder of what came to be known as the Democratic Socialist Party, and later served as Dean of the College of Comparative Law of Soochow University. Following the outbreak of the Sino-Japanese War, he was successively member of the People's Political Council, the Political Consultative Conference, and the National Assembly. In the National Assembly he had a key role in drafting the Constitution of 1947. Despite his outspoken criticisms of Chiang Kai-shek's "personal government," Chang believed during the post-war years that, in view of the prevailing political conditions, more could be accomplished by trying to reform the government from within than by working from without. In the following selection, Chang voices with characteristic frankness his opposition to dictatorship and his belief in constitutionalism, as well as his disillusionment with Chiang's psychological and mental make-up.

THE part which Chiang Kai-shek has played in the history of modern China will be a subject of heated controversy for a long time. As successor to Sun Yat-sen he enjoyed the unique distinction of being able to bring China under his unified control. . . .

. . . A good deal of controversy arose within the party on the question of political tutelage. As part of the plan made by Dr. Sun it sounded well enough, but it was difficult to put it into practice without danger of evolving toward totalitarianism. As generally understood, the purpose of tutelage was to train the people in the practice of running a democratic government. But how was this to be done? How long should tutelage last? Chiang himself threw some light on this matter in his book *China's Destiny:*[1]

According to the steps outlined in "The Plans for National Reconstruction" the period of tutelage follows the military stage, and the chief task is to introduce self-government. The criterion for the practice of self-government is based on the Regulations for the Practice of Local Self-government drawn up by Sun Yat-sen. Constitutional government depends upon the result of the practice of local self-government. The steps in this program are clear and logical and provide no grounds for controversy.

But for years after the removal of the capi-

---

[1] This book was published in Chinese in 1943 but was not rendered into English until 1947. [Editor's note.]

Carsun Chang, *The Third Force in China* (New York: Bookman Associates, 1952), pp. 90–108, 237–39. Reprinted by permission.

tal to Nanking circumstances hindered progress in the basic task of political tutelage, from both the practical and the theoretical side, the question of how to carry out the work of political tutelage became a controversial issue and the question of how long this period of political tutelage should be continued was also hotly debated. Such dissension not only provided the feudalists and counter-revolutionists with pretexts for opposing the government, but also gave comrades within the party, the appearance of wavering, with the result that arguments became more numerous, and there was no unity of action. We all know that political tutelage is the path that must be followed to attain democracy, without which the people's rights cannot be protected, and that otherwise the constitution to be framed in the future can only be a worthless piece of paper.

Here is a question of life or death for the Kuomintang and Chiang Kai-shek. If the aim of the Kuomintang members was democracy, they should have had confidence in the people and ruled in accordance with the general principles of a constitutional government based upon the sovereignty of the people. After the end of the Northern Expedition, which was the end of the military stage, they should have started introducing the constitutional stage immediately, following the schedule laid down by Dr. Sun — military government, tutelage, constitutional government. But Chiang is a soldier; his view was that the intermediate stage should be prolonged as much as possible. The other Kuomintang leaders saw the situation differently; men like Wang Ching-wei and Hu Han-min had their own interpretation of Dr. Sun's plan. They had been just as close to Dr. Sun as Chiang Kai-shek, if not closer, and they thought that they knew Sun's mind better, a claim which was not in fact extravagant. Political tutelage implies the training of the people for constitutional government. If this is accepted, then the practice of parliamentary rule and its attendant privileges and responsibilities, should have been introduced forthwith. These institutions are as essential in the cultivation of democratic virtues as is the swimming pool for one who is to be trained as a swimmer. So long as there are merely lectures on swimming for the swimming class, and no swimming pool, how can the student learn to swim? The Kuomintang, in the first ten years of its existence under the direction of Chiang Kai-shek, never allowed or legalised the existence of opposition parties. For my part, I do not see how an opposition party can get its necessary training except under a constitutional government which granted it equal rights with the party in power.

The people of China waited for twenty long years before the first election of the legislative assembly finally took place in 1947. Since the people never had any experience of elections during all these years, how could they be expected to vote intelligently when the election actually took place? The result was that the Kuomintang, still under the name of tutelage, kept the political power for itself alone. They talked much about local self-government, because, under the cover of local government, they could increase the number of their party members, whom they expected to appoint to all the offices in the villages; it was their aim to accomplish this and then announce that the stage of constitutional government could begin. This was Chiang's interpretation of political tutelage, and here lay the roots of internal conflict later experienced by the Kuomintang. So long as there was no constitutional government, those who controlled Kuomintang policy with regard to military, financial, and diplomatic policy, would appear to the elements not in power, and even to Kuomintang members, as arbitrary and dictatorial. Chiang, as the leader of the ruling group, held the reins of the party and government and grew in personal power. Since Chiang's powers grew in this manner, it is no wonder that provincial governors like Li Tsung-jen,[2] Pai Chung-

[2] Li Tsung-jen was governor of Anhwei Province in 1938, but he more frequently operated from his home base in Kwangsi Province. [Editor's note.]

hsi,[3] Feng Yu-hsiang,[4] and Yen Hsi-shan,[5] rebelled against him. Chiang was a dictator in the eyes of these men, and when they opposed him he called them feudal-minded counter-revolutionists who were trying to overthrow the established government.

So long as there was no constitutional government, there was no parliament, no responsible cabinet, no freedom of the press and no freedom of association. Naturally opposition to Chiang's regime grew, and the Chinese Communists contributed to it, even though their own government was organised on a completely dictatorial basis. The democratic parties which really fought for democracy were then willy-nilly maneuvered into a position in which they had to side with the Communists against the government, when they could have given all their support to the government. It is a pity that Chiang lost the sympathy of large sections of the Chinese people by stubbornly refusing to give up his authoritarian government. This situation inevitably bred corruption and incompetence in the government, and when it was charged with these vices by people both within the country and abroad, there was nothing to say in its defense.

Even as late as the time when Chiang wrote *China's Destiny*, where he said, "We know that tutelage is the path that must be followed," he still firmly believed in his authoritarian views. By that time a good deal of damage had already been done. But Chiang seemed to be indifferent to or unaware of the evils of tutelage. Truly, as

Lord Acton said, "Power corrupts and absolute power corrupts absolutely."

Chiang Kai-shek may have thought that he was dealing cleverly with his internal enemies, but he should have realised that so long as the opposition had just grievances and the people refused to support him, he would find it difficult to tackle the two major international issues which came to a head between 1931 and 1937. One was the question of Japan, and the other that of the Soviet Union's active support of the Chinese Communists. Chiang was sandwiched between these two enemies. The Japanese continued to take Chinese territory. First they seized Mukden and the other cities in Manchuria after having expelled the Chinese forces. In the next year they established "Manchukuo," which declared its independence from China. In 1933, Japan invaded Jehol and created a demilitarised zone in Eastern Hopei. In 1935 Japan went further and tried to create an autonomous North China.

Chiang was then called a traitor because he did not declare war against Japan. In the meantime the Chinese Communists got ahead of him and launched an anti-Japanese campaign in 1935. If Chiang fought against Japan, as the Communists demanded, he was afraid that the Communists would fish in troubled waters and extend their influence at his expense — which in fact they did from 1937 till the Japanese surrender. Chiang declared many times that he was preparing for war, but still made no decisive move — a policy which was in a sense justified because he knew that he was not fully prepared for a full-scale struggle with Japan. In the eyes of the Chinese Communists, Stalin was justified in signing a Mutual Non-Aggression Pact with Nazi Germany, but when Chiang Kai-shek wanted to wait one or two years in order to insure military preparedness before taking on Japan, they called him a traitor. Stalin could sign an agreement for the partitioning of Poland, but Chiang Kai-shek was not granted more time to prepare for a war of self-preserva-

[3] Pai Ch'ung-hsi, also of Kwangsi, is a close ally of Li Tsung-jen and an outstanding military strategist. He never held provincial governorship. [Editor's note.]

[4] Feng Yü-hsiang (1882-1948), the noted Christian General, was military governor of Honan and Shensi before the Northern Expedition. [Editor's note.]

[5] Yen Hsi-shan (1883–1960) was appointed Military Governor of Shansi Province in 1912 and its Civil Governor in 1917. In 1918 he was officially designated the "Model Governor" by the Peking Government. With or without the governorship, he was for decades the effective authority in Shansi. [Editor's note.]

tion. Chiang became increasingly embarrassed by the Communist-launched anti-Japanese campaign. But he kept quiet and bore the humiliation stoically even during the period of his kidnapping in Sianfu.[6] It was not until a year and a half later when the Marco Polo Bridge incident occurred,[7] that he decided to declare war against Japan. . . .

. . . And how the nation rallied round him, as he fought singlehanded, without any foreign assistance! With his stern will and self-discipline to provide the example, the people willingly and joyfully bore enormous sacrifices without so much as a whimper. All this is to the eternal credit of Chiang Kai-shek, and no Chinese would deny that in those days he was at the pinnacle of his prestige as a leader and patriot.

What was the reason for [the] deterioration and collapse? The question has often been asked, and will no doubt continue to be asked by future historians. My own answer can be summarized in one little word — "tutelage": it is as simple as that. Tutelage meant in practice the desire of the Kuomintang's followers to perpetuate the conditions which placed political power in their own hands. They merely gave lip-service to constitutionalism as a sop to Dr. Sun's followers and to show that his teaching was not forgotten. Since there was no constitution, no parliament, and no responsible cabinet, all questions of defense, finance, and diplomacy were decided by the party. The people had no right to question the party. While the war was going on, Chiang Kai-shek was elected Tsung-Tsai, or Director-General of the Party,[8] and his power became unlimited. Any expenditure which was approved by him was legally valid. He issued orders by means of notes in his own handwriting. In Chungking, Chiang's government was

openly called "the note-writing government," and the system naturally led the way to a whole crop of abuses. Any minister who was in Chiang's favor — and this was especially true of Chen Li-fu — could go to his office and get a large sum approved for expenditure. Those ministers who were not close to him had to suffer. Tutelage, in the end, was not even rule by the party as a whole but degenerated to rule by personal whim. Chiang is a man who has confidence only in his relatives, in his brothers-in-law H. H. Kung and T. V. Soong and their subordinates, in the Chen Brothers,[9] and in Chen Cheng, the present Prime Minister of Formosa.[10] Though there was a People's Political Council[11] which was supposed to serve as an open forum for discussion, yet when there was any question raised about the military or financial condition of the country, it was shouted down by the Kuomintang members, who preserved their majority by unconstitutional means. The opinions of the liberals and the opposition parties never had a chance to be heard.

It is natural enough that the absolute power of the Kuomintang led to abuses and rampant corruption. The Kuomintang has never had a record of sponsoring efficient government. . . .

. . . Because there was no parliament, no official media of publicity, no check, and no accountability on the part of ministers, nothing could be done to stop the abuses. If someone had the courage to write an article in the newspapers about these cases of corruption, he was regarded as one who wilfully tried to undermine public confidence in the government, and he courted great personal danger. Is it not obvious that in this species of political tutelage lie the roots of demoralization and

---

[6] Chiang Kai-shek was kidnapped by his troops from Manchuria on December 12, 1936, and released on Christmas Day. [Editor's note.]
[7] July 7, 1937. [Editor's note.]
[8] Chiang Kai-shek was elected Director-General of the Kuomintang in 1938. [Editor's note.]

[9] Ch'en Kuo-fu (1892–1951) and Ch'en Li-fu (1900–   ). [Editor's note.]
[10] General Ch'en Ch'eng, Vice-President of the Republic of China, resigned his concurrently held post as President of the Executive Yuan in December, 1963. [Editor's note.]
[11] The PPC was in function from 1938 to 1948 as "an organ of national opinion." [Editor's note.]

corruption of the government and the army?

Chiang is not a man who abides by law or believes in the rule of law. How much he respects constitutional practice can be gathered from the following remarks which he made in the early years of the republic to the party members of the Kuomintang:

Attention was generally centered on the text of the provisional constitution in the belief that, if only a system of responsible government could be enforced, Yuan Shih-kai[12] could be prevented from abusing his authority as President. They also thought that if a powerful political party could be organised to control the parliament, a responsible cabinet could be maintained to carry out the task of restricting the authority of the President. They also copied the form of British and American politics, believing that if two major parties existed side by side, the mould of democracy would have been set.

Chiang then concluded by saying that

What Yuan Shih-kai feared was not the parliament, but the influence of the revolutionary party in the Yangtse Valley and the Southern Provinces.

By "influence" Chiang meant the governors who commanded the army. Constitution and parliament in Chiang's mind are tools which can be manipulated. He does not believe in the inviolability of a constitution decided on and promulgated by the people. He does not understand why there should be so much fuss made over the constitution. To him all government is personal government: constitutions are luxuries which at most serve the purposes of the one who is in power. During the tutelage period, constitutional amendments were made with regard to the position of the Chairman of the Chinese Republic. When Chiang was himself the Chairman[13] he gave himself real power in the constitution with regard to policy making. When later Lin Sen was Chairman of the Republic,[14] he became a mere figurehead and the real power went into the hands of the President of the Executive Yuan — who was Chiang himself. The constitution was simply remade to fit the changed circumstances. Chiang regards all institutions with complete indifference, being certain that he can manipulate them in any way he chooses. Imagine having more than 3700 members of the National Assembly, which is the constitutional organ that elects the President and the Vice-President of the Chinese Republic! When the Communists were in Chungking, Chou En-lai and myself were both opposed to such an unwieldy number, but the Kuomintang insisted on having it or there was to be no agreement. When the National Assembly actually was in session in 1947, its operations proved to be most awkward and difficult, which was a foregone conclusion. And Chiang never appears to think that laws representing the popular will should be carefully observed; he changes them when they do not suit him. I remember well that, after the rules concerning the People's Political Council were published, when the number of candidates was found to exceed the number fixed, he just increased that number to suit his purposes. Laws are only putty, to be moulded into any shape and form according to the mood of the moment, and that is how China was governed in the most critical period of her modern history, threatened by a large-scale foreign invasion on the one hand and by the determined expansion of the Communists on the other.

Such is the balance sheet of Chiang's personal character, of his strength and weakness. It is possible that he is not this kind of person by nature, that he is the product of circumstances; these, however, are all of his own making. The fact remains that his self-established rule gives encouragement to the sycophants, flatterers, and

---

[12] Yüan Shih-kai (1859–1916) was President of China from 1912 to 1916. [Editor's note.]
[13] Chiang was Chairman of the State Council from 1928 to 1931. [Editor's note.]

[14] Lin Sen was President of China from 1931 until his demise in 1943. [Editor's note.]

toadies by whom he is surrounded, and that he spurns men of integrity, honor, and ability who, out of self-respect, cannot remain in the company of these shameless hangers-on — or, if they do, must sooner or later fall victim to their wiles and intrigues. This is not to deny that Chiang has his greatness. As a fighter on the battle-front, as a revolutionist executing the will of Dr. Sun, and as a leader in the war of resistance against Japan, he made a great contribution to China, and he will be remembered, accordingly, as a patriot. While the early attempt at collaboration with the Communists was one fraught with difficulties, Chiang managed to pull through; when his government ultimately collapsed in 1948–1949, its failure was due not so much to lack of American support, as it is still widely but erroneously believed in America, but to its inherent defects, deriving very largely from the peculiar characteristics of Chiang's personality and his methods of rule. . . .

. . . He believes that he is the only one to carry out Dr. Sun Yat-sen's will. He thinks that Sun's doctrine should be followed as strictly as Leninism and Stalinism are in Soviet Russia. Chiang does not realise that, while the Soviet Union imposes Leninism and Stalinism upon its people, the Conservative Party in Great Britain has never had a book called "Conservatism," or the Liberal Party a book called "Liberalism," or the Socialist Party a book called "Socialism." The Conservative, Liberal, and Socialist parties study the real situation in the political and economic field and try to find a remedy for it in their own ways. They have their party programs, which are revised from time to time. But the Generalissimo knows so little about how the Western democracies work, and runs his own government on such narrow party lines and on the basis of his personal likes and dislikes, that it is impossible for him to see things objectively. What are the departments of a government for? To look after the interests of the people. Why are there civil servants in each ministry? To run the ministry efficiently. What is a currency system for? It is the medium of economic exchange, and should be kept stable in order to avert economic hardship. But such concepts, elementary as they are, are beyond Chiang's comprehension.

What the Generalissimo did was to try to impose the party on every institution. Education to him was training the students to be Kuomintang members, not training them to be good citizens. The Examination Yuan and its training corps do not work for the improvement of the civil service but try to make young men into loyal party members. The currency system, after it was changed over from a silver-based system to that of a managed currency, had tided over China's financial difficulties during the war period; but Chiang had the idea that because China is a rural and not an industrial country, it could not suffer economic collapse even if there was super-inflation. He expounded this idea on many occasions. Even with the experience of the inflation during the war, he never believed that it could drive the country, including business people, the salaried class, and the soldiers, into ruin. I have never known a mind more unsuited to cope with the problems of the modern world. Personal power is all that Chiang understands. Under such leadership, how can there be an efficient government in China — let alone a constitutional government?

. . . Chiang's government has been guided entirely by his whims and arbitrary decisions made on the spur of the moment. He sees no need for any system or organization. Under such a regime, the art of government becomes, for all practical purposes, the art of studying the infinite variety of his moods; it produces two kinds of government officials, those who have won his favor and those who have not — or, in other words, those who are always prepared to say "yes" to whatever Chiang may say, and those who believe in independent thinking, personal integrity, and personal dignity. The yes-men are those who win his favor, the flatterers and sycophants who would not utter a critical word in any gathering over which Chiang happens to preside. This was what happened when war was declared against Germany. The meeting over which the Generalissimo presided and which was attended by the ranking officials of the government, was a meeting of silence. Only the Chairman of the government, Mr. Lin Sen, dared to speak, and what he said was that the document before the meeting should be sent to his office to be signed! It is said that a house must have solid foundations before it can stand. The government of Chiang Kai-shek was built on quicksand and clay. How can it stand? Is it any wonder that it fell like a house of cards when it had to face the Communist crisis?

Military Rule and National Ruin

CH'IEN TUAN-SHENG

Professor Ch'ien Tuan-sheng (1899—   ) has been a close observer and occasional participant in the Chinese political scene since receiving his doctorate in government at Harvard in the 1920's. A member of the wartime People's Political Council and of several missions to the U. S., he has also held academic and political posts in Communist China as President of the College of Political and Juridical Sciences in Peking, Vice-President of the China Association of Politics and Law, delegate to the Chinese People's Political Consultative Conference, and member of the Central Committee of the Democratic League. Professor Ch'ien, however, is best known as a leading professor of political science in China's major universities. His careful analysis of the ancient Confucian principles, of Sun Yat-sen's hopes and failures, and of the competing constitutional devices and party cliques within the Kuomintang has cast a new light on the collapse of the Kuomintang regime and the rise to power of the Chinese Communists. In this article, written during his Visiting Lectureship at Harvard in 1948, he expresses his profound disillusionment with and vigorous objection to the supremacy of the military in the Kuomintang government. But if his conviction in civil supremacy in government caused him in 1949 to cast his lot with the Communists, in the belief that it was necessary to foster another powerful political group in order to check the military, his thought reform in 1951–53 and again in 1957–61 is perhaps evidence enough of his essentially liberal proclivity.

O NE of the significant differences which distinguish good governments from bad is the subordination of military power to political power and of military personnel to political personnel. The military mind tends to be narrow and irresponsible. Militarists may be experts, but their expertise often prevents them from giving due weight to interests other than military. Military power, unless kept in its proper place, usually runs amok and takes the whole country with it.

The misfortune of modern China is that, at the time of the multitude of paper reforms which enshrouded the country in the first decade of this century, she should have entertained a serious liking for the military institutions of Prussia and Japan. The Prus-

Ch'ien Tuan-sheng, "The Role of the Military in Chinese Government," *Pacific Affairs*, XXI, No. 3 (September 1948), pp. 239–51. Reprinted by permission.

sian tradition had been adopted whole-heartedly by the receptive Japanese *samurai* when the Japanese looked to the West for instruction. When the time came for China to look abroad, she adopted the military institutions of Japan and Germany.

Chiang Kai-shek's indispensability to the Kuomintang was initially of a purely mili-tary nature. He owed his rise to the fact that he was a military man. As such, he was made head of the Military Academy and later appointed Commander-in-Chief of the Revolutionary Army. After the con-clusion of the Northern Expedition he was regarded as the man who would be able so to reorganize the Army as to rid the nation of the curses of militarism and war-lordism. Had he done so, he could have become a far more effective political leader. But he did not do so.

The nearest approach to a powerful check on military power in China since the Revolution of 1911 was the reorgan-ized Kuomintang in its early years. But when Chiang Kai-shek acquired a position of leadership in the Kuomintang without at the same time outgrowing his military mentality, the Party ceased to be such a restraining influence. Even had the anti-militarist members and factions of the Kuomintang wished to impose a continued check on the military, the latter, headed by Chiang Kai-shek, had become too pow-erful to suffer effective restraint.

From 1925 to 1946 the Military Com-mission of the National Government was almost uninterruptedly in existence and had charge of the nation's military affairs. When the Commission was first set up in July 1925, a few days after the estab-lishment of the National Government it-self, it was put directly under the guidance and supervision of the Party and was en-trusted with the administration and com-mand of all of the armed forces and mili-tary organizations. It was conceived strictly as a committee in form as well as in spirit. At that time, it was one of the three great governing organs established by the Central Executive Committee of the Kuomintang, the other two being the Political Committee and the Government Committee.

When the Northern Expedition began, the Military Commission was reorganized. Although still possessing the highest powers of military organization and administration, it was placed under the Government. The committee spirit was retained. But the be-ginning of the Northern Expedition also saw the creation on July 7, 1926, of the post of Commander-in-Chief of the Na-tionalist Revolutionary Army, outside of the Military Commission. Chiang Kai-shek was appointed to this post and was authorized to act concurrently as Chairman of the Military Commission. . . .

. . . The two years of the Northern Ex-pedition culminated in Chiang Kai-shek's military supremacy. Whether, at the end of the Expedition, he enjoyed that suprem-acy in his capacity as Chairman of the Military Commission or as Commander-in-Chief of the Revolutionary Army was im-material. Merely to abolish the General Headquarters would have been of no sig-nificance; had the civilians wished to regain control over the military, something more fundamental would have had to be at-tempted. But all attempts have hitherto failed.

The Military Commission of the Na-tional Government was reestablished in March 1932, in theory as a corporate body. In regard to organization and training of the forces and other general military poli-cies, the Commission was to act as a com-mittee and the powers of the Chairman were to be restricted to those of a presiding officer. Only when in command of actual military operations was the Chairman to receive the powers usually delegated to a commander. . . .

The organization and powers of the Mili-tary Commission were more clearly defined by the Organic Law of the Military Com-mission of January 17, 1938. The Chair-man became Commander-in-Chief of the armed forces and was empowered "to direct the people of the whole nation for the purpose of national defense." The original corporate character of the Commission was abandoned, and the Chairman was made superior to the whole body. Under this law, Chiang Kai-shek acquired high powers necessary for conducting the war against Japan.

The Military Commission consisted of from seven to nine members, most of whom concurrently headed the more important establishments of the Commission. Although these establishments were, generally speaking, all military in nature, the functions of the Commission were not confined to military matters. At one time it included a Commission for War-Zone Party and Government Affairs, which had, theoretically at least, most extensive political powers. At another, its Bureau of Transport Control was empowered to fix transport priorities and even to control some means of transportation directly. At all times the Political Department, charged with indoctrination of the armed forces, civilians and enemy prisoners, ostensibly to prosecute the war, embarked upon all kinds of cultural work and duplicated many of the undertakings of the Publicity Department of the Party and the Ministry of Education of the Executive Yuan. In addition, an Office of Councillors delved into economics, finance, general administration and foreign affairs. In the determination of foreign policy, they frequently overshadowed the Foreign Minister.

The Aides to the Chairman were, even more, confidential assistants and advisers, and therefore also more influential. They were in charge of military intelligence and espionage, kept personal records of prominent persons in all walks of life (which gave them the power to censor or recommend all appointments to Chiang Kai-shek in his multifarious capacities of leadership), and screened the individuals and the information which were to reach him. It must be remembered that, of the various high Party and Government posts held by Chiang Kai-shek during the war, the Chairmanship of the Military Commission was considered by himself and by the public alike to be the most responsible. It was in that capacity that he was both addressed and spoken of, and material reaching him or appointments made with him, in whichever of his various capacities, were generally channeled through the Office of Aides. Legally, the Chairman was the head of the military establishment and was charged with responsibility for conducting the war. But extralegally, if not illegally, the Chairman had all other powers conferrable by the Party or the Government. He could have exercised his non-military powers in his other capacities. To the extent that he chose, as he often did, to act through the Military Commission, he sacrificed observance of the law to expediency.

It is obvious that inability to put the military in its proper place has plagued China during the last generation. That the Chinese army has been ill-disciplined and badly organized is equally obvious. A measure of neutralization, which would release the armed forces from personal and partisan loyalties and other political biases, is recognized as constituting the first prerequisite for the improvement not only of the forces themselves but also of the general administration.

The Ministry of National Defense was . . . established on July 1, 1946, superseding the Ministry of Military Affairs. The various departments and establishments of the Military Commission were either dissolved or absorbed by the new Ministry. The Army, Navy, Air Force and Supply Force were organized as parallel services, and were brought under the command of the Chief of the General Staff, who is responsible to the Minister. Each of the four forces has a commander-in-chief, but the Chief of the General Staff, assisted by deputy chiefs for each force, has power over all of them in matters of strategy and tactics.

. . . The device should have succeeded

in subordinating the military to the civil authority. But such has not been the result. To date, the Minister has always been a military man. The head of state, whether as President of the National Government or as President of the Republic under the Constitution of 1946, has, since the reorganization, been as eager to exercise personally the powers of command as he was when Chairman of the Military Commission. In other words, the military organization has been somewhat simplified by the substitution of a Ministry of National Defense for the complex mechanism of the previous decades, but the irresponsible use of military power has remained unchanged. No civilian authority has recovered an effective check on military power.

The supremacy of the military creates problems in all spheres — political, constitutional and administrative — not to mention the effect of a large army on the national economy.

Aside from the fact that it has an all-powerful leader in Chiang Kai-shek, the Kuomintang is disrupted by its inclusion of a number of factions. The military group, centered on graduates of Whampoa, is not the only faction and has in fact not been the most powerful; but because the Whampoa Group controls the armies of the Kuomintang Government, it has been an important factor in the disunity of the Party. . . .

Constitutionally, domination by the military is always a danger. It negates the true spirit of constitutionalism. In a constitutional government political parties must have untrammeled freedom to oppose one another without resorting to war, the people must have their rights adequately protected by the courts against all violators, and the assembly elected by the people must be all-powerful in the expression of the wishes of the people. But when the military becomes dominant, the parties cannot oppose each other without fighting real wars, the courts cannot do anything

against the military, and the wishes of the people's representatives do not prevail. . . .

Administratively, military domination enfeebles the civilian authorities. The secondary role of the Executive Yuan in relation to the Military Commission needs no further emphasis. As a matter of fact, military interference in civilian administration is not nearly so bad in the central government as in the local, where the domination of the military has prevented the development of decent and orderly administration. It is noteworthy, though entirely understandable, that the few — indeed, very few — better provincial administrations which the Chinese have experienced during the last two decades have without exception been under civilian leaders who happened to be strong enough to withstand military interference.

The economic consequences of military domination are equally disastrous. One result has been disproportionate military expenditures. Ever since the establishment of the Kuomintang regime, when expenditures could be roughly known, half or more of the total annual budget has always been spent in military items, to the detriment of services of a more constructive nature. Defenders of military expenditures of course argue that unavoidable wars, both civil and foreign, have necessitated them. But the sad thing is that in China the military men, restrained neither by law nor by a sense of responsibility for the popular welfare, have always found wars to be necessary, and these "necessary wars" have constantly depleted the coffers of the state and wrought desolation on the countryside. Has there been since the establishment of the Republic any war except the war against Japan which has been popular and for which money has been willingly spent by the people?

There can be no salvation for China until the military is brought under proper control. . . . If it is necessary to have a powerful political group to check the military, such a group must be developed. Or, if a mass force is necessary for the purpose, such a force must be organized. For, unless the military is confined to its proper place, orderly government is impossible. Proper control of the military may not mean instant realization of orderly government, but orderly government is dependent on proper control of the military. China has suffered at the hands of the militarists in the recent past and still suffers today. She will continue to suffer unless a future regime is able to dominate instead of be dominated by the militarists.

Want of Power and Authority

ALBERT C. WEDEMEYER

General Albert C. Wedemeyer (1897–) succeeded General Joseph W. Stilwell in October 1944 as Commanding General of American forces in the China Theater and concurrently as Chief of Staff to Chiang Kai-shek. His return to the U. S. in 1946 was soon followed by an appointment in 1947 as Special Envoy to conduct a six-week survey of conditions in China and Korea. After his report of September 19, 1947, to the President was suppressed on the ground that its publication would have been highly offensive to Chinese sensitivity, Wedemeyer became persuaded that his mission had been simply another attempt of his government "to provide justification for continuance of the old disastrous China policy." He has since expressed strong disapproval of Marshall's policy of coalition government for China and of Stuart's friendly relations with Chinese leftists, asserting that his personal experiences in China have long convinced him of the subservience of the Chinese Communists to Russian interests. He has also explained that the criticisms of the Kuomintang's corruption and maladministration which he made before an assemblage of ranking Chinese officials during his fact-finding mission would not have been voiced had he known his government's lack of genuine interest in the Kuomintang government. The Kuomintang's outstanding need, he says below, was to secure more power and authority to act effectively, not to institute more political reforms.

O<small>N</small> November 18, 1946, I gave a lecture at the National War College in which, after carefully outlining my experiences in the China Theater, I said:

These experiences taught me that the Chinese situation was capable of rapid improvement. . . . We learned that the Generalissimo and his associates can and will co-operate. They can and did improve the condition of their armies and people. They made rapid strides when they had the benefit of friendly and concrete American advice.

Taking issue with General Marshall and State Department policy, I went on to say that, in my opinion, the Generalissimo could make progress toward the unification of China and the constitutionalization of his government, "if he had realistic American aid — not measured by its bulk but by the wisdom with which it is applied and offered."

Chinese complexities, I said, were compounded by a full-scale, name-calling — and sporadic-shooting — civil war. "We

From *Wedemeyer Reports!* by General Albert C. Wedemeyer, pp. 370–77, selections. Copyright © 1958 by Albert C. Wedemeyer. Reprinted by permission of Holt, Rinehart and Winston, Inc.

are told," I continued, "that the General-issimo and his Kuomintang Government are totalitarian, corrupt, and oppressive, and that the Chinese Communists are dem-ocratic in their agrarian economy and po-litical organization." I admitted that there were elements of truth in these reports, but that they did not give a true picture of the situation in Asia.

It had been obvious to us who were there that, at the time when Japan surrendered, China would be confronted with many grave and pressing problems, not only be-cause of the terrible devastation and dislo-cation of her economy during eight years of war and occupation by the Japanese, but also because of the "deeply rooted internal problems and bitter hatreds and political calumnies that had their inception twenty-five years ago."

Taking issue with General Marshall's analysis of the situation in China, I con-tinued as follows:

The question is often asked: Are the Chi-nese Communists real followers of the doc-trines of Karl Marx? The basic tenets of Karl Marx have undergone many changes in their interpretations and applications, even by Lenin and Stalin. Outside of Soviet Russia one finds marked differences in the tactical implementation of communism by individuals, groups, and political parties that definitely claim allegiance to the ideologies of the Krem-lin. One must watch the basic doctrine and not be misled by local or transitory applica-tions. The Chinese Red leaders themselves state plainly that they find their lives to have meaning only in the context of contempo-rary communism. I am certain that the Chi-nese Communist movement follows the Mos-cow line from week to week, insofar as con-ditions permit. One has only to read the regulations of the Chinese Communist Party to confirm the fact that the fundamental phi-losophy and aims of the Chinese Communists differ very little if at all from their Com-munist brethren the world over. There are striking diversities in application, but defi-nitely no real differences in ultimate objec-tives. I have talked often with the Chinese Communist leaders, Mao Tse-tung and Chou En-lai, particularly with the latter, who speaks

English. Their loyalties are first in the in-terest of Stalin and his program and then in the welfare of their own countrymen.

*   *   *

I added that the Chinese Communists were "not presently emphasizing the appli-cation of the Soviet economic system," be-cause their immediate objective was "to obtain political control"; and that therefore they did not for the moment "hesitate to use certain democratic methods to further attainment of their ultimate goal."

In this same lecture I said that, although the Nationalist Government of China was frequently and derisively described as au-thoritarian or totalitarian, there was a basic difference between it and its Communist enemies, since the Kuomintang's ultimate aim was the establishment of a constitu-tional republic, whereas the Communists wanted to establish a totalitarian dictator-ship on the Soviet pattern. In my two years of close contact with Chiang Kai-shek I had become convinced that he personally was a straightforward, selfless leader, keenly interested in the welfare of his people, and desirous of establishing a constitutional government according to the precepts of Sun Yat-sen. This was obviously impossible so long as China was fighting first the Japa-nese and then the Communists backed by Soviet Russia. "One man alone cannot solve the complexities of China," I subsequently stated, in answer to a question. "I can only assure you that the Generalissimo is sin-cere; that he is a real Christian gentle-man, and I have never found him guilty of artifice or subterfuge. He was always straightforward with me."

Chiang Kai-shek's gravest weakness, it seemed to me, was his loyalty to friends and old supporters. Among his coterie of advisers there were both unscrupulous and incompetent men. If he could not be per-suaded to remove them, it was difficult to conjecture how the situation in China might develop. I had myself pointed out to him that many of his officials were so incompetent or dishonest that the fine program which he visualized for his people could never be accomplished so long as he retained them. For his coterie of officials prevented him from contacting and winning the support of many of the most patriotic and capable men in China. I recognized the fact that Chiang was politically astute, had a logical mind and force of character. However, it also seemed to me that he was weighted down by the Confucian philosophy which required loyalty to family and friends. He had alienated some of the best and most able men in China by his refusal to jettison the cliques around him.

The Generalissimo, in my view, was further handicapped by "the appalling deficiency of trained administrators and technicians." Eighty per cent of the Chinese people were peasants, and it would be difficult even to estimate the degree of illiteracy. There was a thin crust of extremely wealthy Chinese, a very small white-collar class, a small middle class, and a great mass of people living in abject poverty and ignorance. All the difficulties which confronted a Chinese government endeavoring to lift China out of age-old poverty, unite her, and enable her to progress had been immensely aggravated by the cruel and devastating eight-year war against Japan, and subsequently by Communist depredation and destruction. Asking China to reform and democratize her government in these circumstances was like telling a man in the midst of a hurricane that he ought to repair and paint his roof.

In the question period that followed my lecture, I remarked that the process of reform in China would of necessity be slow, and said:

We Americans are impetuous. We are efficient. The British are, too. We see the goal and we want to attain it. We are intolerant of delays and circumventions. Often I would establish objectives that I wanted to accomplish. I recommended them to the Generalissimo, but there would be discouraging delays. I had to continually check myself. The cadence and methods of life in China are not going to be changed radically or quickly. You gentlemen are familiar with European history. You know that hundreds of years were required there to formulate and then implement the Bill of Rights and to create constitutional government. They are passing through a period of transition in China, passing from a feudal or medieval condition, gradually, toward modernism. The degree of accomplishment and the rate at which they move forward will be influenced by many imponderables, intangibles, and unpredictable influences from within and from outside China's borders.

Our stake in China, I said, is just as important and has similar basic justification as our European stake. "The same basic philosophy behind our interests and behind our participation in Europe pertains to the Far East."

I also reminded my National War College audience some twelve years ago that, in determining policy and attitude toward the Generalissimo and his government, we should not forget or lightly dismiss the fact that during the war Chiang Kai-shek had on numerous occasions rejected very favorable terms of peace offered by Japan. If these terms had been accepted, approximately one and a half million Japanese troops would have been released for employment against Americans in the Philippines, the Bonins, the Marianas, and the Ryukyus. The Generalissimo's adamant refusals and firm loyalty to his pledge to fight on with his Allies had "saved countless American lives and naturally contributed to our final victory."

I concluded by saying that, since the U.S. objective in China was to assist the Chinese people in establishing a unified democratic country, thus insuring our own interests in China and in other parts of the world, we should take appropriate steps, including . . .

. . . the deployment of military forces to insure that no other nation or group of nations will attempt to interfere with the realization of our aims. . . .

A realistic approach to the current situation

in the Far East requires our immediate and continued support of the Generalissimo and his government. We should continue economic assistance in the form of loans and supplies, accompanied by appropriate safeguards to insure that our aid is employed for the purpose we intend.

We were insisting that Chiang both institute democratic reforms *and* collaborate with the Communists. We said we wanted a strong and independent China but refused the Nationalist Government the material and political aid and support without which it could not crush the Communists.

The reforms we kept urging the Nationalists to institute would have been hard enough to carry out in peacetime even with U.S. aid, and were totally impossible in the midst of the civil war, which was in fact a Sino-Russian War.

China's real need was for a government with the power to govern. As I saw it the worst ills of China — corruption, maladministration, inefficiency, and the like —

were the result not of the dictatorial nature of its government but of its lack of power and authority to get its orders carried out. And Chiang Kai-shek could to some extent, although not entirely, be excused for his failure to clean up his administration by having all along had his hands tied both by the endless war and his need to retain loyal cadres if China was not to fall apart. To call Chiang Kai-shek a fascist dictator, as was the fashion in America, was a ridiculous reversal of the truth, but was tragic in its consequences since it led to U.S. policy being based on a false premise. The powers of the Chinese Nationalist Government, far from being totalitarian, were much too limited. It interfered with the individual too little, not too much. Its sins of omission, not of commission, were the cause of its eventual downfall. Its gravest defect was the ineffectiveness of its administration and its consequent failure to enforce reforms which were all beautifully worked out on paper and decreed.

Failure in Land Reform

PING-CHIA KUO

Ping-chia Kuo (1908–   ), teacher, publicist, and civil servant, has taught in Chinese and American universities. His public career has included appointments in the Chungking government as Counselor of the National Military Council, Counselor to the Ministry of Foreign Affairs, and Chief of the Editorial and Publication Department of the Ministry of Information. His book on the history of modern China, from which this selection is taken, stresses perspective rather than the mere collation of facts. Regarding history as being "determined by the powerful economic and social forces," Professor Kuo ascribes the collapse of the Kuomintang to its "fatal weakness" in not being willing to effect land reform and its inability to elicit support from either the landed gentry or the peasantry. Thus, Kuo differs in interpretation from Carsun Chang, Ch'ien, and Wedemeyer. Chang and Ch'ien criticize the Kuomintang's tutelary or military dictatorship because they believe it to be structurally or theoretically unsound. Kuo, more interested in political analysis than in political theory, questions the soundness of the Kuomintang tutelage when it is programmatically without reference to China's social and economic problems. Devoid of social change, Kuo says, Chiang's China was hardly in a position to deal effectively with the Communist challenge. To Wedemeyer, the answer is more authority and power for the government; to Kuo, it is the fulfillment of the "basic needs" of the people.

THE course of history in China, as indeed in any other country, is actually determined by the powerful economic and social forces that affect the fortunes of the people as a whole. Despite the vicissitudes of forty centuries, the evolution of Chinese society and economy, particularly of the problems and needs of the masses, forms a continuous thread of change, which alone can explain the events of our time.

It is in the light of this process of economic and social revolution that the current upheaval may be assessed in proper perspective. The rise of the Communists to power is no isolated event. Certainly it is not merely the work of a group of revolutionary extremists. Its roots reach far back into the structure of the old society, the abuses of government, the inequalities and miseries suffered by the people, and a widespread demand for change.

It was against this background that the Revolution of 1911 was launched and the Republic brought into being in 1912. The great beacon light during this epoch was Sun Yat-sen. The next twenty years may well be called the Age of Sun. From the historian's standpoint, Sun is the crucial bridge linking the *ancien régime* with the impending onslaught of the Communists. He was prophetic enough to sound the warning and to show the road to constructive action. But as he fathered and revitalized the Kuomintang revolution, he was caught in the vortex of all the retarding influences of dissolution. Following the founding of the Republic, Sun and his colleagues plunged into a veritable "mass of loose sand." The old regime had collapsed, but amidst the debris the conservative forces remained intact. . . .

The two decades of General Chiang's ascendancy were marked by a great concentration of the nation's energies and resources in maintaining the Kuomintang position by means of military and political power, to the neglect of the economic and social program, which, in fact, was the only program that could give it real strength. A great hue and cry was raised about Kuomintang tutelage, which was to introduce preparatory steps for democracy. The campaign for the abolition of the unequal treaties was pushed with great publicity. But neither drive had any substantial success, because the basic needs of the people were not met, and the government consequently could not achieve that real strength which could come only from nationwide support. What the nation really witnessed was the use of great military power by General Chiang to enforce the authority of Nanking, and the struggle of the politicians and the privileged groups to gain power and to promote their respective interests. Thus unification was only nominal. Regional warlords openly challenged the central government. The party was torn by factional strife, as secession movements appeared time and again in the southern capital of Canton.

The degree to which the government remained fixed in its indifference to the needs of the masses was indeed astonishing. It showed a strong desire for reconstruction and modernization, but whatever progress was made in this direction was intended primarily to strengthen the power of the ruling circles. As far as the fundamental problem of the well-being of the masses was concerned, it had neither the resolve nor the drive to tackle it. The cause of this withering of the revolutionary spirit was the inability of the government to bridge the gap between itself and the bulk of the population in the countryside. As in earlier ages, the Kuomintang ruled the countryside through an alliance with the landlord class. At this telling level of government — from the hsien (county) downward into the villages — all power, political, economic, judicial, and police,

Reprinted from *China: New Age and New Outlook* by Ping-chia Kuo, pp. 3–4, 17, 25–30, 79–80, by permission of Alfred A. Knopf, Inc.

was in the hands of the landlord class. The Kuomintang depended on their co-operation to collect taxes, to maintain order, and to direct the village government. On the two counts that vitally affected the masses — taxation and local village government — there was neither justice nor popular representation. But most serious of all was the failure of the Kuomintang to carry out an effective program for land reform. From all available evidences, the Kuomintang had a great opportunity to put land reform into effect. Had it done this, it would have won the support of the masses, and true unification and peace would have followed. But the groups in control were opposed to social change. Without social change there could be no improvement in the standard of living of the people. This was the fatal weakness of the Kuomintang government.

. . . Land reform did indeed receive the attention of the legislators. The law passed by Nanking provided for the lowering of farm rents to 37½ per cent of the crop yield, the abolition of subtenancy, and the right of perpetual lease. But it remained on the books without being enforced. The landlords continued to collect rents which ranged as high as 50 to 70 per cent, exacting as much as they could get. The impact of this state of affairs on the peasant population was far-reaching. For the government to pass a progressive measure and then fail to keep its pledge to the people by enforcing it appeared to be adding insult to injury in the eyes of the masses.

. . . The Communists, by watching the Kuomintang performance, found that to grope within the limitations set by Kuomintang methods would not meet the needs of the people. In an underdeveloped country like China, the quest for democracy of the Western type provided no safeguards against abuse by the leaders in power and could only result in continuing the empty forms of the preceding years. They further believed that the power structure in Nanking, a repetition of the evils of past dynasties, would only worsen with time, as the clash of the Kuomintang dictatorship and the interests of the masses came into sharp focus. The basic trouble with the Kuomintang, in their opinion, was that all its efforts were directed toward a struggle for power within the privileged groups, while the land and peasant problem, the most urgent of all revolutionary tasks, was left untouched. Such insight into the logic of the times molded a new body of revolutionary ideas and tactics in the minds of Mao and his associates. Within a surprisingly short period of time, these crystallized into a program of action whose central thesis — directly opposed to that of the Kuomintang — was that the only potential base for an effective revolutionary government was in the vast agricultural population. Accordingly, without losing time, the Communists set out to put their program to a practical test in the agricultural heartland of central China.[1]

The result was immediate and startling. The latent power in this great human reservoir responded almost instantly to the tapping by the Communist leaders. They quickly discovered that not only could they regain the ground lost in 1927 but they could expand their strength on a vast and lasting basis by focusing all strategy to accord with their new insight into the almost limitless explosive force in the economic and social revolution. In the agrarian revolution they launched in the rural border areas of Kiangsi and Hunan, the peasants were given a leadership and an organization that were without precedent in history. Grievances were actively built up against the village bosses as well as against the rule of the gentry in combination with the *tangpu* (local Kuomintang party headquarters), the telling level at which the Kuomintang failed to offer a satisfactory program to the masses in the countryside. After the existing power structure was broken, the Communists organized local government by soviets, wherein the poor and landless peasants were given the major

[1] In Kiangsi Province under the leadership of Mao Tse-tung and Chu Teh, dating back to 1928. [Editor's note.]

voice; they distributed land taken from the landlords to this rural proletariat. Most important of all, along with these radical reforms, the peasants were organized into a Red Army. This welded together the Communists' political and military power and created an integrated weapon of assault for the emancipated peasants as a class against all the privileged groups of the country.

The fact that the Communists were able to achieve so swift a victory [after 1945] is viewed by certain quarters as a near miracle. The truth of the matter is that they won on two counts. For one thing, they did not act with haste in the battlefield. The strategists took time to plan their moves. As a result, they did not have to decimate every Kuomintang division but rather compelled most of them to desert or surrender. There was no seesaw battle; the Red legions rolled on from one major theater to another in rapid succession. Whatever battles they fought struck at the vital perimeters of Kuomintang defense so that isolated pockets of resistance could have little meaning. Another reason for the speedy victory of the Communists — and this is even more significant than the former — was the loss by the Kuomintang of the support of the village gentry and city merchants. The economic deteriora-

tion and government fumbling from 1947 onward were such that a general atmosphere of despair enveloped the classes which were the customary pillars of the Kuomintang government. The Kuomintang forces had to join battle with the enemy like lone battalions, denied the support of the groups of which they were the avowed champions. This was a direct reversal of the situation created in the years of the Taiping Rebellion, just about a century ago. The times, both then and now, were periods of great storm and stress. Both actions were centered in the trans-Yangtze regions. But while Tseng Kuo-fan could create fresh units of *"hsiang-yung"* ("village braves") to fight the Taiping rebels because he had the solid support of the gentry, General Chiang Kai-shek in 1947–9 found it hard to rally the gentry to his cause. For twenty years Chiang had stood for the landlord and the privileged classes; but in this hour of need, they failed to respond to his call. Such was the futility of his policy that he had to throw the Kuomintang army, otherwise magnificently supplied and equipped, into what was obviously a lost struggle. The victory of the Communists was thus in the last analysis due to the prostration of the Kuomintang brought on by the falling away of its habitual sources of support.

CHINA IN WORLD POLITICS:
THE CHALLENGE OF
INTERNATIONAL COMMUNISM

Stalin's Grand Strategy

HU SHIH

Hu Shih, (1891–1962), a student of John Dewey and a leading liberal educator in China, was instrumental in setting in motion, in 1917, the Chinese literary renaissance which brought about the recognition and general adoption of the living spoken-language as the tool of literature and education. He was professor and dean at the National Peking University, where he also served as chancellor in 1945–49. This educator's role, together with his service as Ambassador to the U. S., gave him a close association with official circles as well as public forums. To the end of his life, he remained a paragon of the independent intellectuals who belonged to no party, no clique. Yet in the world-wide struggle between democracy and communism, he felt impelled to make a political choice, and his return to Formosa in 1958 to assume the presidency of Academia Sinica was the result of such a decision. Here Dr. Hu expounded a widely held view that the Kuomintang debacle was the product of twenty-five years of Stalinist intrigue.

IN the following pages I propose to study Stalin's grand strategy of world conquest as it can be discerned in China — its stages of experimentation and modification, of successes and failures, and its victories after long failures. The story covers 25 years, from 1924 to 1949, and culminates in the recent and, I trust, temporary conquest of continental China by the overwhelming military power of world Communism. I propose to use the history of the long and bitter struggle between Nationalist China and world Communism, between Chiang Kai-shek and Stalin, as source material for a new examination of that almost unbelievably successful strategy which has enabled world Communism to place under its domination immense areas of the earth and 800,000,000 of its population.

All the strategical elements . . . present in the Eastern European conquests . . . are present in the Asiatic conquests. There is always the Communist Party in full strength; there is always the maximum aid including armed force from the "base of Socialist revolution;" and there is, above all, the objective condition of revolution, namely, the greatest war in human history.

But there seem to be other equally important elements not revealed in a documentary research which can be clearly seen in a comparative study of the many Communist conquests extending from the Baltic Sea to China and Korea. First, it is not

Hu Shih, "China in Stalin's Grand Strategy," *Foreign Affairs*, XXIX, No. 1 (October, 1950), pp. 11–40.

enough to have the conscious leadership of the Communist Party. To be an effective instrumentality of conquest, the Party must be fully armed: it must have a strong army of its own. Second, it is not enough to use Soviet Russia as a base for revolution. It is necessary first to make Soviet Russia the greatest military Power in the entire world, and then to achieve "revolutionary" conquests of adjacent and contiguous territories by sheer overwhelming superiority of military strength. Third, to avoid the appearance of "overt violence" or "revolutionary violence," it is necessary to bring about a "coalition government" with all the "democratic" and "anti-Fascist" parties or groups in a country. And lastly — and above all — there is the strategy of deceit which has been best expressed by the great Lenin: "We must be ready to employ trickery, deceit, lawbreaking, withholding and concealing truth."

There is one historical fact which differentiates the Chinese Communist Party from the Communist movements in any other country outside of Soviet Russia — a fact which is essential to a clear understanding of what has been happening in China during the last quarter of a century. It is that the Chinese Communist Party, partly by design and partly by extraordinary historical circumstances, has possessed a formidable army of its own almost from the very early years of its founding. . . . This unique feature of the Chinese Communist Party has been the most important source of its strength, which Stalin, the masterful strategist of world Communism, has been able to nurture, support, and in the course of 25 years develop into a most powerful instrumentality for subjugating China and thereby dominating the whole Asiatic continent.

Among the 21 "Conditions of Admission to the Communist International," adopted at the Second World Congress of the Comintern, July–August 1920, the fourth condition reads: "Persistent and systematic propaganda and agitation must be carried on in the army, where Communist groups should be formed in every military organization. Wherever, owing to repressive legislation, agitation becomes impossible, it is necessary to carry on such agitation illegally. *But refusal to carry on or participate in such work should be considered equal to treason to the revolutionary cause,* and incompatible with affiliation to the Third International."

Since no country under normal conditions will permit either revolutionary propaganda and agitation in its army or the organization of an armed force by a revolutionary party, it was a most extraordinary opportunity for the Third International to be requested in 1923–1924 by Dr. Sun Yat-sen, leader of a revolutionary party and many times head of an independent regional government, to send political and military experts to China, not only to help reorganize his own party, but actually to organize a new army for a new revolution. It was equally extraordinary for Dr. Sun Yat-sen, in his sincere desire to "bolster the strength of revolutionary elements in the country," to admit Communists as regular members of his own Nationalist Party, thereby making it possible for Communists to influence the policy of the Nationalist Party and even to carry on revolutionary propaganda and agitation in the new army.

The Chinese Communist Party, founded in 1921, had already affiliated itself with the Communist International. The three years of collaboration between the Kuomintang and the Chinese Communist Party (1924–1927) formed the period when the Comintern was making full use of a most unusual opportunity to try out its strategy of world revolution on a large scale in one of the most important strategical areas of the world — China.

This was the time when Stalin was formulating his thesis of the consolidation of Soviet Russia as the base for world revolution, a thesis which never meant abandonment of the cause of world revolution in favor of "Socialism in one country" but only emphasized the importance of effective aid

that could come from a strong base. A
political struggle for power was then going
on in Russia between Stalin and Trotsky,
but Stalin was already in full control of
the policies of the Comintern. There is
little doubt that Stalin was directing the
Comintern's China adventure throughout
those years of Nationalist-Communist collaboration.

Then came the great crisis of the revolution. On March 24, 1927, Nationalist
troops entered the city of Nanking after the
flight of the northern forces, savagely attacked foreigners in the city, looted and
defiled foreign dwellings and consulates,
and killed a few of the foreign residents,
including the vice-president of the American missionary University of Nanking.
Foreign gunboats stationed in the river
were forced to fire a barrage to warn
against further violence and to guide the
fleeing foreigners to escape to the boats.
. . . It is quite probable that the Nanking affair of March 24 was a deliberate
strategical move to involve many foreign
Powers in armed intervention. . . .

This danger of foreign intervention and
a Communist Revolution was averted by
the decision of Chiang Kai-shek and the
moderate leaders of the Kuomintang to
"split" with the Communists, end the collaboration, and "purge" the Nationalist
Party of the Communists and their sympathizers. The "purge" began on April 12,
1927, in Shanghai and later in Canton. On
April 18, Chiang, with the support of the
Elder Statesmen of the Party, set up the
National Government in Nanking.

After the moderate wing of the Kuomintang had brought about the "split" and the
"purge" in the lower Yangtze Valley, and
had set up the National Government at
Nanking, the Kremlin sent a secret message
to Borodin[1] in Hankow ordering the Chinese Communists to demand majority control of the Kuomintang, confiscation of land
of the landowners and the formation of a
separate Workers' and Peasants' Army.

. . . Even the Left Wing Kuomintang
could not tolerate such open violation of
the terms of the collaboration. Borodin and
the other Russian advisers were expelled
from the Party and ordered to leave China.
Eventually the Hankow régime collapsed
and was merged with the Government at
Nanking.

It is significant that the organization of
a Chinese Workers' and Peasants' Red
Army was actually ordered by the Kremlin
and therefore constituted a part of the
strategy of Stalin. And the order was carried out by those Communist leaders and
army commanders — Chu Teh, Ho Lung,
Yeh T'ing, Mao Tse-tung, Li Li-san and
others — who wanted to carry on the Chinese Communist Party but who realized
that, after the 1927 coup d'état, the Party
must have an armed force of its own. It
was these men who started the Nanchang
Uprising on August 1, 1927, and the Autumn Crop Uprising in Hunan in September, and who after their defeat and retreat
into the mountains, pooled their remnant
forces to form the first Red Army.

Early in 1930 a Provisional Soviet Gov-
ernment of Southern Kiangsi was pro-
claimed.[2] In August 1931, the Executive
Committee of the Communist International
advised the Chinese Communist Party to
establish in some secure region a full-
fledged "central Soviet Government" and
to carry out a "Bolshevik national policy."
Such a "Central Soviet Government of the
Soviet Republic of China" was set up in
December 1931,[3] with its capital at Juichin,
Kiangsi, near the border of Fukien. Mao
Tse-tung was elected Chairman of the
Central Soviet Government, and Chu Teh,
Commander of the Red Army.

From 1930 to 1934, the National Government forces under Generalissimo Chiang
Kai-shek carried out a number of military
expeditions against the Communist armies. . . .

[1] Michael Borodin was Soviet political advisor to
the Kuomintang. [Editor's note.]

[2] Kiangsi Provincial Soviet Government, founded
in February 1930. [Editor's note.]
[3] The Soviet Republic of China was founded on
November 7, 1931. [Editor's note.]

The encirclement and the economic blockade proved so effective that the Red Army and Government were forced to adopt the bold strategy of retreat — to escape annihilation by retreating westward, then southwestward, then northward, and then northeastward, finally reaching their destination in northern Shensi. This retreat has been called "the Long March," which lasted for a whole year and covered about 6,000 miles.

. . . In later years when Chinese Communists could freely associate and converse with their non-Communist friends it was reliably reported that leading Communists attributed the success of the Long March to what Stalin had taught as "the strategy of retreat." For it was Stalin who, in his best known work, "Problems of Leninism," had laid down the strategical line of "a manœuvring of reserves designed for a correct retreat when the enemy is strong and when retreat is inevitable, when we are beforehand aware of the disadvantages of engaging in battle which the enemy imposes on us, when, given the ratio of forces, retreat is the only means of preventing a blow on the vanguard and of maintaining the reserves behind it." . . . "The object of this strategy," concludes Stalin, "is to gain time, to decompose the enemy, and to assemble forces so as to take the offensive later."

So, according to my source of information, it was this Lenin-Stalin doctrine of "correct retreat" that had influenced the military thinking at Juichin in 1934 and had resulted in the Long March and the survival of the Red Army.

Stalin and the Communist International were then to play another and even more important rôle in protecting and preserving the Red Army strength and providing it with ample opportunities for growth and expansion. The new strategical line was to be the "united front."

Even when the Red Army was fighting its way to the northwest, the policy of the Communist International underwent an important change. The Seventh World Congress, held in Moscow from July to August 1935, officially proclaimed the policy of a "united front" against the rising dangers of aggression by the "Fascist" Powers. . . .

Under this new party line, the Chinese Communist Party was organizing all kinds of front organizations such as "The Association for National Salvation and Resistance to Japan," "The People's United Association against Japan," and so on. These associations were carrying on antigovernmental agitation under the cloak of anti-Japanism. They demanded immediate war against Japan and immediate cessation of the civil war against the Communists. . . .

It was against such a background that the "arrest" of Chiang Kai-shek by Chang Hsueh-liang took place in Sian on the morning of December 12, 1936. . . .

. . . Why was Chiang Kai-shek able to fly back to Nanking on Christmas Day? What had happened to make that possible? . . .

. . . I am inclined to think that, in the light of the future trend of events, Stalin's strategy was probably greatly influenced by his solicitude for the future of the Chinese Red Army, which, we must remember, was one of his own creations. . . .

From one of the secret pamphlets issued by the Chinese Communist Party after the Sian affair we can learn that there was so much criticism and dissatisfaction after December 1936 that explanation "lectures" had to be prepared in order that the Party and the Army might fully understand the action at Sian. In these secret explanations, it is interesting to note that the central argument was that the Party must obey the directives of the Comintern which were motivated by considerations for the "larger benefits" and "greater victories" in store for the Communist Party. . . .

So once more it was Stalin's strategy which brought about a peaceful settlement of the Sian Affair and saved the lives of Chiang Kai-shek and practically all his highest ranking generals.

The Generalissimo returned to Nanking amidst the really spontaneous rejoicings of the Chinese people. He left Sian without having to sign any terms. But this Puritan Christian was won over, probably for the first time in his life, by a masterful stroke of strategy. Of all the things Stalin has ever done, that act came closest to statesmanship. The Generalissimo felt reassured that he could take in the Chinese Communists as partners in the common fight against the Japanese aggressor. The war for the extermination of the Red Army was ended. The Red Army was saved.

Seven months later, in July and August 1937, China took up the fight against Japan. The Second World War, which had actually started on September 18, 1931, in Manchuria, and which Chiang Kai-shek had for six years tried to avoid, often under most humiliating circumstances, was now in full swing.

Another month later, in September 1937, the Red Army was incorporated as the Eighth Route Army of the National Army. It was now sent to the war front in Shansi, where it looked forward to a future of unlimited growth and expansion.

. . . Soviet Russia tried to act properly during the years of the war: the military supplies under the Sino-Soviet barter arrangement were delivered to the Central Government. The amount of ammunition that could come through from Soviet territory to the Communist area in the northwest must have been very small.

Then came the sudden end of the Pacific war in August 1945. On August 9, Soviet Russia declared war on Japan. On the same day, the Soviet Army began to move into Manchuria. On August 14, Japan surrendered. Air landings of Soviet troops were made at Mukden, at Kirin, and at Changchun. Before the end of August, Soviet Russian troops were in complete control of Manchuria — of its railroads, of the great naval base of Port Arthur, of the great port of Dairen, and of all the other ports and cities.

With the invading Soviet armies there also came the Chinese Army that had been organized on Soviet soil out of different Chinese detachments which had left Manchuria in the 1930's. . . .

The Soviet Army did not withdraw until the end of April 1946. During the nine months of occupation in Manchuria, every facility was given to the Chinese Communists, while serious obstacles were placed in the way of Nationalist troops that were being slowly transported into Manchuria with the logistical support of the United States Government.

Out of Manchuria, Communist armies, newly equipped and reconditioned, were pouring into Shantung across the sea, and into North China by land. By September 1948 Shantung was lost. By November, Manchuria was lost. By early 1949, North China was lost. Through a most astute and wicked stroke of strategy, Stalin had taken Manchuria and made it the contiguous base for the new military strength of Chinese Communism, behind which lay the unlimited support of Soviet Russia, now the mightiest military Power in the whole world.

A conference of the Big Three had been held at Yalta in February 1945. The conference lasted seven days. At one of the very last sessions, Prime Minister Churchill was not present, and President Roosevelt, according to Harry Hopkins' record, "was tired and anxious to avoid further argument." At this meeting, Stalin proposed the conditions for Soviet Russia's entry into the Pacific war. The resulting agreement was kept secret from China until June 14 when Ambassador Hurley informed Generalissimo Chiang Kai-shek in Chungking that on February 11, 1945, Roosevelt, Churchill and Stalin, on behalf of their Governments, signed at Yalta a secret agreement. . . .

That Stalin was deliberately deceiving and blackmailing Roosevelt, I have not the slightest doubt. For years past, Stalin and Molotov had taken every occasion to impress on the American leaders that Soviet Russia had no interest in supporting Chinese Communists, because they were not Communists at all. The Soviet leaders had insisted that Chiang Kai-shek was a great man and deserved support, and that the United States must take a leading part in giving aid to China. Molotov in August 1944 even told Ambassador Hurley and Mr. Donald Nelson the "inside" story about the Generalissimo's imprisonment at Sian in December 1936, and assured them that it was "the political and moral support of the Soviet Government" that saved Chiang's life and returned him to the seat of his government.

Henry Wallace, Hurley and Hopkins had all told President Roosevelt of this friendly concern and political and moral support which Soviet Russia and Stalin had for Chiang Kai-shek. In the Department of State version of the Yalta Agreement on the Far East, there is a very revealing footnote which quotes Ambassador Harriman's comment on the clause relating to the "lease of Port Arthur as a naval base of the U.S.S.R." Mr. Harriman says: "I believe President Roosevelt looked upon the lease of Port Arthur for a naval base *as an arrangement similar to privileges which the United States has negotiated with other countries for the mutual security of two friendly nations.*"

Such, in brief, is the story of the unfolding of Stalin's strategy of conquest in China. The heart of this strategy has been the creation, preservation and nurturing to full strength of the Chinese Red Army. It has taken nearly a quarter of a century for the Red Army to achieve sufficient power for the conquest of continental China. This Red Army was many times defeated, broken up and nearly annihilated by Chiang Kai-shek's armies; and Stalin and world Communism might never have succeeded in China if the greatest war in human history had not intervened.

The pattern of conquest is therefore the same in China as in Poland, Bulgaria, Hungary, Rumania, Jugoslavia and Czechoslovakia. It is the pattern of conquest by force and violence projected from the contiguous Russian base. What seems to differentiate China from the seemingly much easier conquests in Central and Eastern Europe has been the much greater complexity and difficulty of the conquest, which made it necessary for Stalin to resort to the most cunning forms of secret diplomacy in order to overcome the resistance that Nationalist China had been able to summon for over two decades.

Communist Subversion and American Appeasement

ANTHONY KUBEK

Professor Kubek, a graduate of Georgetown University and now Chairman of the Department of History and Political Science, University of Dallas, holds America responsible for the "sovietization of China and Manchuria." He shares the views of men like General Patrick J. Hurley (Ambassador to China in 1944–45), William C. Bullitt, and Congressman Walter H. Judd in regarding the Chinese civil war as a manifestation of the worldwide struggle between America and the Soviet Union, between freedom and enslavement. The Chinese people and the Kuomintang government, he says, had the will to resist Communist onslaught; but the American government, whose policy and action could have made the difference between a hopeless and an effective resistance, withheld both timely aid and moral support. While President Roosevelt, President Truman, Secretaries of State Marshall and Acheson, and Secretary of the Treasury Morgenthau were not personally guilty of Soviet sympathy, they

must bear the final responsibility for the "sorriest chapter" in America's foreign relations for having placed themselves under the decisive influence of
Soviet sympathizers, "extremists," and even known Communists. As a result
of their indiscretion, the Department of the Treasury, during the Second World
War, formulated policies "designed to insure economic collapse" of the Kuomintang government, and the State Department, until the inauguration of the
Eisenhower administration, had virtually nothing save "public and private
vilification" for a deserving ally. In sum, Kubek explains "the whole story of
the greatest mistake of a century" in terms of two alleged policy errors of the
American government: the decision to seek a coalition government between
the Kuomintang and the Chinese Communist Party, which, he quotes Mac-
Arthur, had "just about as much chance . . . as that oil and water will mix";
and the refusal to render "such assistance to the conservative Government of
China" as was necessary to stem the tide of Chinese Communism.

EXCEPTING only the meeting at Teheran, the one at Yalta, in the
Crimea, was the most important international parley since the peace conference at
Paris in 1919. And judging by its results
one may say that history has repeated itself.
President Roosevelt was out-traded and out-
maneuvered by Stalin, just as the prag-
matic-minded statesmen of Europe dealt
with President Wilson. Roosevelt pinned
his hopes on the curative potentiality of the
United Nations organization as Wilson did
with his League of Nations. Europe, which
at the Paris Peace Conference sold out
idealism and principle for territorial greed
and a punitive peace, finally produced an
embittered Germany that accepted Hitler
as a better alternative than the misery and
chaos of economic ruin forced upon her by
excessive reparations. The League proved
powerless to correct the mistakes of the
Versailles Treaty. The same thing has been
in evolution now with the United Nations
which has been powerless to correct the
mistakes of World War II.

But the primary responsibility for the
policies which characterized our wartime
diplomacy must rest with Roosevelt who,
far more than any other American President, directed the conduct of our foreign
relations. Under the influence of Soviet
sympathizers and reinforced by his own
eagerness to please Stalin, no one in the

country was more thoroughly deceived by
Russian promises than Roosevelt. He was
obsessed with the idea that through a personal meeting with Stalin he could mold
the pattern of international relations in the
form that was closest to his heart's desire.

It is glibly asserted by many die-hard
New Dealers that there was no alternative
to the policy of Soviet appeasement. Regarding this assertion two questions may
fairly be asked. First, did the Soviet record
before the conferences at Teheran and
Yalta suggest that a dominant position for
the Soviet Government in Europe and Asia
would promote the interest and security of
the United States? Second, were voices of
warning raised, pointing to the probably
grave consequences of acquiescing in the
annexationist ambitions of a regime with
unlimited aspirations for world domination? The answer to the first question is an
emphatic "No." The answer to the second
question is an equally definite "Yes." Before
the Yalta Conference, which took place
early in February, 1945, there were no less
than eight major actions of the Soviet
Union, well known to official Washington,
and which should have inspired grave
doubts as to Soviet intentions and good
faith. Surely these "Stop, Look and Listen"
signs should have been heeded by American negotiators at Yalta. But some of these

Anthony Kubek, How the Far East Was Lost: American Policy and the Creation of Communist
China, 1941–1949 (Chicago: Henry Regnery Co., 1963), pp. 88–89, 98–99, 177–79, 407–10, 448,

advisers were strongly pro-Soviet, looking forward to a close association between Stalin and Roosevelt in determining the condition of the postwar world. They were eager to push Roosevelt into the hungry arms of Stalin who had his own ideas about world domination.

The secret briefing papers . . . which the President took with him to Yalta contained the Department of State's views on the Far East. These briefing papers clearly reflected an official apprehension about the future of Russian-American relations in that part of the world, but which Roosevelt's conversations at Yalta did not reflect in the least. Roosevelt may never have seen these briefing papers. He told Stalin that he blamed General Chiang Kai-shek more than "the so-called Communists" for the failure to gain a coalition government. Stalin replied that "new leaders" were needed around Chiang Kai-shek.

If [Alger] Hiss at the time of the Yalta Conference was still under orders of the Communist apparatus, which is entirely possible, it is not, then, [il]logical to suspect that copies of our preparatory documents for the Yalta Conference might have been immediately channeled to Soviet representatives in Washington, to be forwarded to the Kremlin. Roosevelt was then a very tired and enfeebled man who before, during, and after the Yalta Conference seemed to be in a perpetual hurry to get things done no matter how (admittedly not even looking at the carefully prepared briefing papers). Is it not at least a strong possibility that, prior to the Yalta Conference, Stalin and Molotov familiarized themselves with our American background and program documents while the President of the United States neglected to do so? Is it not quite possible that our Soviet antagonists knew of our moves beforehand — that they knew what points of our program they would attack before Roosevelt knew that he was going to make those points? If the Soviet Union had advance access to our positions and policies, we would be like a man playing poker with a mirror at his back. His opponent could see his hand before the play began.

How important was Alger Hiss at Yalta? Hiss himself answered that question when he testified before the House Committee on Un-American Activities. Here are some key questions by Congressmen Karl Mundt of South Dakota and answers as they appear in the official record at the hearing:

MR. MUNDT: Did you participate in the Yalta Conference?

MR. HISS: I did, Mr. Chairman.

MR. MUNDT: Did you draft or participate in the drafting of parts of the Yalta agreement?

MR. HISS: I think it is accurate and not an immodest statement to say that I did to some extent, yes.

A bit later in the hearing, Mundt asked Hiss if he had participated in drawing up the veto provisions that later were to appear in the United Nations charter. This colloquy developed:

MR. MUNDT: What I was trying to get to is whether you participated in the creation of the draft.

MR. HISS: I did participate in the creation of the draft that was sent by President Roosevelt to Churchill and Stalin, which was the draft actually adopted at San Francisco.

MR. MUNDT: Did you lend your influence in the direction of having the veto provision included in that draft?

MR. HISS: I did. That was practically the unanimous position of the American government, I might add.

Why, after repeated disclosures concerning the Communist activities of Alger Hiss, did our top officials insist on including him in the delegation at Yalta? Whittaker Chambers in his book[1] says he told about Hiss in 1939 to Assistant Secretary of State Adolph Berle, who talked to President Roosevelt about it. In another instance, Martin Dies, former chairman of the House Committee on Un-American Activities, says that Roosevelt and his key aides in 1941

---

[1] Whittaker Chambers, *Witness* (New York: Random House, 1952).

did not believe the list of about two thousand Communists on the federal payroll, including Alger Hiss. But in spite of these grave revelations about Hiss, his name was placed in the list of delegates to the Yalta Conference.

. . . Beginning in the 1930's, the United States Treasury Department became one of the most heavily and decisively infiltrated of all departments of the U. S. Government. This group exercised almost complete control in the Treasury Department during the early 1940's. During the period of 1944–1946, another shift in direction of Communist infiltration occurred. The United Nations, its Specialized Agencies, and organizations such as the International Monetary Fund became gathering points for Communist agents who flocked from various agencies of the U. S. Government. Most of the key agents in the Treasury Department moved to the International Monetary Fund and to various agencies of the United Nations. Apparently they felt that the monetary and economic affairs of the United States had become so enmeshed in the workings of international organizations that the most decisive influence could be exercised at the international level. Also, in view of Congressional investigations and other exposures of Communist activity, international agencies offered a far safer haven than agencies of the United States Government. However, it would be naive to suppose that the Communist apparatus would put all its eggs in one basket. Indeed, more recent disclosures have shown that the Soviets by no means abandoned infiltration of our government agencies.

During the war years — a period in which monetary matters were of critical importance to the government of China — a group of Soviet agents in the Treasury Department enjoyed dominant influence in monetary matters of the United States and also over economic aspects of the prosecution of the war. Heading this group was Dr. Harry Dexter White. White was a brilliant intellect, an outstanding economist, an expert in monetary matters, and

an exceptionally gifted organizer. He joined the Treasury Department on June 30, 1934. His rise was rapid, and he soon became the dominant influence in that department. On March 25, 1938, he became Director of Monetary Research. On August 30, 1941, White was appointed Assistant Secretary of Treasury, in charge of all monetary affairs. In 1945, the Director of Monetary Research under White was V. Frank Coe, identified by Elizabeth Bentley as a member of the Silvermaster group. Coe's assistant was Dr. Harold Glasser, identified by Elizabeth Bentley as a member of the Perlo group. Thus, by the end of the war, the monetary affairs of the United States were virtually in the control of the Communist apparatus.

It was this group of men that made the decisions bearing on the financial stability of the Chinese Government. They had the power and the resources to stabilize the Chinese currency and preserve the Government of China — or to debauch the currency and overthrow that government. In line with Soviet policy, they took the latter course.

Much light has been cast upon the manner in which these Soviet agents in the Treasury Department established policies designed to insure economic collapse of the Nationalist Government of China. It should be pointed out that these people, in many instances, operated directly contrary to the policies and orders of President Roosevelt. They so misled and befuddled Secretary of the Treasury Henry Morgenthau, Jr., as to render him totally ineffectual. In the case of President Roosevelt, he was often led to believe that the course of action being taken was the opposite of that actually taken by White and his associates. Congress was in much the same position. Nothing indicates any personal responsibility of President Roosevelt with regard to the contrived economic collapse of the Chinese Government.

Aid to China was one of the most perplexing and controversial problems confronting the United States in the postwar period. In general, our policy had long been one of deep interest in maintaining the integrity and independence of China. We regarded her as essential to peace and stability in the Far East. However, there were people in and out of government who had little use for Chiang Kai-shek and his Nationalist government. Our policy became one based on the mistaken belief that the Chinese Communists would bring a new surge of democracy to China. As late as March 11, 1948, General Marshall, as Secretary of State, told a press conference that "The United States . . . still favors a broadening of the base of the Chinese Government to include the Communists." Eleven months later, as the Communists' armies swept toward victory in China, fifty-one Republican members of the House addressed a letter to President Truman on February 7, 1949, inquiring, "What is our policy toward China?" Secretary of State Dean Acheson told them in a private session, on February 24, 1949, that it was the intention "to wait until the dust settles" before deciding upon a policy. But the dust had already settled over unfortunate China — a Red dust.

Both the Chinese people and their leaders had the will to resist the Communists, but what we gave them in the form of aid and moral support was the difference between a hopeless and effective resistance. What amount we did give them in terms of actual aid was "too little and too late" to be of any real use. As a result, Chiang Kai-shek, under the impact of continued Communist military pressure, was forced to surrender one position after another.

Regarding aid to Nationalist China, General MacArthur's testimony is quite pertinent:

SENATOR WILEY: . . . What would you have done — what would you have advised, under the circumstances that existed back there in 1945 — what would you have done?

GENERAL MACARTHUR: I would have given such assistance to the conservative Government of China as to have checked the growing tide of Communism.

A very little help and assistance in my belief, at that time would have accomplished that purpose.

SENATOR WILEY: For a good many years you have been acquainted, I take it, with the Russians and with the Communist infiltration.

Would you have sought to have gotten those two forces together?

GENERAL MACARTHUR: I did not catch the question.

SENATOR WILEY: Would you have sought to have amalgamated the Commies and Nationalists — have gotten them together?

GENERAL MACARTHUR: Just about as much chance of getting them together as that oil and water will mix.

In that colloquy lies the whole story of the greatest mistake of a century. Time alone can show how damaging, how devastating, have been the errors of Teheran and Yalta.

In summarizing the problem of aid to Nationalist China, we should keep certain factors firmly in mind. From the time the China Aid bill was signed by the President on April 3, 1948, to the actual time of delivery, there was a seven months delay, at which time the Communists began their first major successful drive in North China. Those seven months delay were of crucial importance.

The apologists for the strategy of defeat which prevailed at that time talk about how much in dollars was the value of our aid to China. But they do not tell you how much of what was delivered, to whom, when, where, and in what condition. And they do not mention the intangibles, such as moral support and effective training. They have led the public to believe that we gave enormous amounts of aid to China, that it was all wasted, that we did everything we could, that the Chinese Government never took our advice, that the Chinese soldiers had no will to fight — in short, that the Government of China was so bad that there was nothing we could have done that could have saved it. All of these assertions have been proven to be absolutely untrue.

The charge that we did everything we

could is refuted by the plain fact that from VJ-Day until Eisenhower's inaugural address in 1953, very few words of *moral* support from the American Government can be discovered — nothing but public and private vilification. Furthermore, our Government steadfastly refused to give to our military advisors in China the same authority that it gave to Van Fleet in Greece to "advise and train at all levels" — without which authority he could not possibly have succeeded there, any more than without it, our "advisors" could have succeeded in China.

Aid that arrives too late, no matter how much its dollar value, is not real aid. Lend-lease aid that was dumped into the Bay of Bengal was not aid to China, no matter how many hundreds of millions of dollars it figures in the tables of alleged "aid to China." The equipping of Chiang's best thirty-three divisions with American 30-caliber rifles, and then putting an embargo on 30-caliber ammunition — as General Marshall did from the summer of 1946 until at least May, 1947 — is not aid, no matter how much the value in dollars of the rifles. The total operation had the net result of effectively *disarming* Chiang's best troops instead of arming them as Americans have been led to believe was the case.

When 30-caliber ammunition finally was released for China, it was charged against the funds provided by Congress at the rate of replacement costs of $85 per 1,000 rounds, instead of its actual cost to us, on original manufacture, of $46 per 1,000 rounds. But ammunition sent from the same dumps to the Greeks was charged at a "surplus price" of $4.60 per 1,000 rounds. So State Department accounting methods lacked something in the way of honesty.

Refusal to let Chiang get, either by purchase or by grant, aviation gasoline for the planes and air force Chennault had built is not effective aid, no matter how many dollars show up in the tables as the cost of the planes!

Most important of all was the refusal to let our military mission in China give real advice and training to the Chinese armed forces at all levels and in the field. It would be virtually impossible to train any army with a thousand advisers compelled to sit in Nanking working on tables of organization. And, still worse, the refusal to give one word of moral support and encouragement during those long, dreary years did much to bring about the defeat of the Nationalist Government on the mainland. There is no other case in American history where a supposed ally spent several years in vicious vilification of a friend it was posing before the world as trying to help.

In short, what China needed was *proper aid* even more than more aid. *Proper aid* was what our Government systematically, and with apparently malicious forethought, refused to give. If we had treated Greece, Italy, France, or even England the way we treated the Government of China, they probably would have gone down too. It is the sorriest chapter in the history of America's relations with other countries.

The result — sovietization of China and Manchuria — could be the only logical outcome of postwar United States policy toward China. The utter consistency of our policy in serving Soviet ends leaves no conclusion other than that pro-Communist elements in our government and press "planned it that way." But top American officials who sought to buy Soviet cooperation at any price must bear the final responsibility.

It should be clearly evident that the Communists cannot gain the world unless our own government helps them to do it. Soviet agents cannot run the United States government, but their purposes can be accomplished by extremists who are willing to seek accommodation at every turn, and if the aim is the formation of a world "coalition government." The China debacle was not achieved by Communists alone, nor could it have been. The Communist conquest of China was secured by non-Communists who had their own reasons for doing what they did. But it does seem reasonable to suppose that a fanatical extremism equalled only by that of the Communists themselves was at least partially responsible.

The details of the China debacle have been recorded with a fair degree of completeness. As a case study, this episode is of extreme value and significance. As an exposure of the *modus operandi* of Soviet conquest, it can hardly be equalled. The lessons we can learn are vital ones on which our future as a free people could depend. In the case of China, we junked our traditional policy which insisted upon the territorial and administrative integrity of China. There is no doubt on that point.

External Political Influences and
Internal Chinese Forces

DEAN ACHESON

Dean Acheson (1893–   ) was U. S. Secretary of State when he ordered the release of the *White Paper* in August 1949. Published at a time when the fall of the Kuomintang government on Taiwan was generally expected by American policy-makers to occur in 1950, the *White Paper* had the dual purpose of justifying past policy of the U. S. and of cushioning the shock to U. S. prestige in the event of further political reverses in China. In his covering letter to the President, Acheson explains America's continuing interest in China as based on the Open Door Policy of respect for China's administrative and territorial integrity and of opposition to the domination of China by any foreign nation. Specifically, the American government seeks, in the post-1945 period, to achieve two objectives: (1) to help promote a stable, democratic government, and (2) to assist the Kuomintang government in the realization of the first objective. It is for this reason that men like Hurley, Marshall, and Wedemeyer were sent to survey the Chinese scene and to assist in the negotiations between the Kuomintang and the Chinese Communist Party; and Acheson notes, apparently in reply to charges by administration critics, that it was the Kuomintang government that had initiated the negotiations as early as May 1944. Acheson hints at certain possible American errors in judgment, such as placing undue trust in the Chinese Communists' willingness to cooperate with the Kuomintang and in Russia's profession of exclusive support for the Kuomintang government; but he asks the American public to view the administration's record "in the light of conditions prevailing when the events occurred," one of the conditions being the reports by General Hurley, subsequently a vociferous critic of the State Department, that peaceful solution between the Kuomintang and the Chinese Communist Party was possible.

Acheson also discusses the much debated and explosively controversial issue of the secret Yalta Agreement of February 11, 1945, by which the Soviet Union formally committed itself to an early attack against Japan in exchange for America's recognition of Soviet interests in Manchuria, Outer Mongolia and certain other areas. Here again Acheson appeals to the facts as they existed at the time. He emphasizes America's "manifest duty" to win the war as early as possible and with the least expenditure of lives. The atomic bomb was not yet a reality; it was, therefore, deemed "vital" to ensure early Soviet participation in the Pacific War. He further notes that, after Pearl Harbor, the Kuomintang troops had become more interested in gaining a superior position over the Communists than in fighting the Japanese. Hence, while many administration critics decried the Yalta Agreement as a "surrender of principles" and Hu Shih deplored it as another example of Stalin's "strategy of deceit," Acheson describes it as a "price" America had to pay in the vigorous prosecution of the war. In the political decision America had to make in this connection, there was neither surrender of traditional American principles nor sacrifice of basic national interests.

The burden of Acheson's argument is that the American administration had exercised its best judgment under the existing circumstances and that in any event the attainment of peace, prosperity, and stability in China could "in the last analysis . . . be done only by China itself." The Kuomintang collapsed because of the facts that "somewhere" during the decade of 1927– 37 the Kuomintang had lost its "crusading spirit" and hence its people's loyalty; that it failed to implement land reform; that the Second World War had enervated the government "not only militarily and economically, but also politically and in morale"; that Chiang Kai-shek had turned himself away from "unpalatable advice"; that the Kuomintang suffered from military disintegration even as it entertained the "illusion" that the Communist threat could be resolved by force of arms; and that the constitutional government fell short of "a truly national system of government." The situation in China being what it was, the only alternative which could have dislodged the Chinese Communists was to involve America in a full-scale war, an alternative which would not only have met with condemnation by the American people, but would also have "diametrically reversed our historic policy" of Open Door in China.

Viewing history in perspective, Acheson advances the suggestion that China's problem as epitomized in the fall of the Kuomintang government is the product of internal forces arising out of two principal historical factors: population pressure and Western cultural impact. He also voices the hope that "ultimately the profound civilization and the democratic individualism of China will reassert themselves and she will throw off the foreign yoke." In spite of the domination of China by a Soviet inspired regime, the Chinese will remain true to themselves as surely as America will be to her historic friend.

THE PRESIDENT: In accordance with your wish, I have had compiled a record of our relations with China, special emphasis being placed on the last five years. . . .

The interest of the people and the Government of the United States in China goes far back into our history. Despite the distance and broad differences in background which separate China and the United States, our friendship for that country has always been intensified by the religious, philanthropic and cultural ties which have united the two peoples, and has been attested by many acts of good will over a period of many years, including the use of the Boxer indemnity for the education of Chinese students, the abolition of extraterritoriality during the Second World War, and our extensive aid to China during and since the close of the war. The record shows that the United States has consistently maintained and still maintains those fundamental principles of our foreign policy toward China which include the doctrine of the Open Door, respect for the administrative and territorial integrity of China, and opposition to any foreign domination of China. It is deplorable that respect for the truth in the compilation of this record makes it necessary to publish an account of facts which reveal the distressing situation in that country. I have not felt, however, that publication could be withheld for that reason.

The record should be read in the light of conditions prevailing when the events occurred. It must not be forgotten, for ex-

Dean Acheson, "Letter of Transmittal, July 30, 1949," *United States Relations with China* (Washington D. C.: Division of Publications, Department of State, 1949), pp. iii-xvii.

ample, that throughout World War II we were allied with Russia in the struggle to defeat Germany and Italy, and that a prime object of our policy was to bring Russia into the struggle against Japan in time to be of real value in the prosecution of the war. In this period, military considerations were understandably predominant over all others. Our most urgent purpose in the Far East was to defeat the common enemy and save the lives of our own men and those of our comrades-in-arms, the Chinese included. We should have failed in our manifest duty had we pursued any other course.

In the years since V-J Day, as in the years before Pearl Harbor, military considerations have been secondary to an earnest desire on our part to assist the Chinese people to achieve peace, prosperity and internal stability. The decisions and actions of our Government to promote these aims necessarily were taken on the basis of information available at the time. Throughout this tragic period, it has been fully realized that the material aid, the military and technical assistance, and the good will of the United States, however abundant, could not of themselves put China on her feet. In the last analysis, that can be done only by China herself.

Two factors have played a major role in shaping the destiny of modern China.

The population of China during the eighteenth and nineteenth centuries doubled, thereby creating an unbearable pressure upon the land. The first problem which every Chinese Government has had to face is that of feeding this population. So far none has succeeded. The Kuomintang attempted to solve it by putting many land-reform laws on the statute books. Some of these laws have failed, others have been ignored. In no small measure, the predicament in which the National Government finds itself today is due to its failure to provide China with enough to eat. A large part of the Chinese Communists' propaganda consists of promises that they will solve the land problem.

The second major factor which has shaped the pattern of contemporary China is the impact of the West and of Western ideas. For more than three thousand years the Chinese developed their own high culture and civilization, largely untouched by outside influences. Even when subjected to military conquest the Chinese always managed in the end to subdue and absorb the invader. It was natural therefore that they should come to look upon themselves as the center of the world and the highest expression of civilized mankind. Then in the middle of the nineteenth century the heretofore impervious wall of Chinese isolation was breached by the West. These outsiders brought with them aggressiveness, the unparalleled development of Western technology, and a high order of culture which had not accompanied previous foreign incursions into China. Partly because of these qualities and partly because of the decay of Manchu rule, the Westerners, instead of being absorbed by the Chinese, introduced new ideas which played an important part in stimulating ferment and unrest.

By the beginning of the twentieth century, the combined force of overpopulation and new ideas set in motion that chain of events which can be called the Chinese revolution. It is one of the most imposing revolutions in recorded history and its outcome and consequences are yet to be foreseen. Out of this revolutionary whirlpool emerged the Kuomintang, first under the leadership of Dr. Sun Yat-sen, and later Generalissimo Chiang Kai-shek, to assume the direction of the revolution. The leadership of the Kuomintang was not challenged until 1927 by the Chinese Communist party which had been organized in the early twenties under the ideological impetus of the Russian revolution. It should be remembered that Soviet doctrine and practice had a measurable effect upon the thinking and principles of Dr. Sun Yat-sen, particularly in terms of economics and party organization, and that the Kuomintang and the Chinese Communists cooperated until 1927 when the Third International demanded a predominant position in the Government and the army. It was this demand which precipitated the break between the two groups. To a large extent the history of the period between 1927 and 1937 can be written in terms of the struggle for power between the Kuomintang and the Chinese Communists, with the latter apparently fighting a losing battle. During this period the Kuomintang made considerable progress in its efforts to unify the country and to build up the nation's financial and economic strength. Somewhere during this decade, however, the Kuomintang began to lose the dynamism and revolutionary fervor which had created it, while in the Chinese Communists the fervor became fanaticism.

Perhaps largely because of the progress being made in China, the Japanese chose 1937 as the departure point for the conquest of China proper, and the goal of the Chinese people became the expulsion of a brutal and hated invader. Chinese resistance against Japan during the early years of the war compelled the unqualified admiration of freedom-loving peoples throughout the world. Until 1940 this resistance was largely without foreign support. The tragedy of these years of war was that physical and human devastation to a large extent destroyed the emerging middle class which historically has been the backbone and heart of liberalism and democracy.

In contrast also to the unity of the people of China in the war against Japan were the divided interests of the leaders of the Kuomintang and of the Chinese Communists. It became apparent in the early forties that the leaders of the Government, just as much as the Communist leaders, were still as preoccupied with the internal struggle for power as they were with waging war against Japan. Once the United States became a participant in the war, the Kuomintang was apparently convinced of the ultimate defeat of Japan and saw an opportunity to improve its position for a showdown struggle with the Communists. The Communists, for their part, seemed to see in the chaos of China an opportunity to obtain that which had been denied them before the Japanese war, namely, full power in China. This struggle for power in the latter years of the war contributed largely to the partial paralysis of China's ability to resist.

It was precisely here that two of the fundamental principles of United States policy in regard to China — noninterference in its internal affairs and support of its unity and territorial integrity — came into conflict and that one of them also conflicted with the basic interests of the Allies in the war against Japan. It seemed highly probable in 1943 and 1944 that, unless the Chinese could subordinate their internal interests to the larger interest of the unified war effort against Japan, Chinese resistance would become completely ineffective and the Japanese would be able to deprive the Allies of valuable bases, operating points and manpower in China at a time when the outcome of the war against Japan was still far from clear. In this situation and in the light of the paramount necessity of the most vigorous prosecution of the war, in which Chinese interests were equally at stake with our own, traditional concepts of policy had to be adapted to a new and unprecedented situation.

After Pearl Harbor we expanded the program of military and economic aid which we had inaugurated earlier in 1941 under the Lend-Lease Act. That program . . . was far from reaching the volume which we would have wished because of the tremendous demands on the United States from all theaters of a world-wide war and because of the difficulties of access to a China all of whose ports were held by the enemy. Nevertheless it was substantial.

Representatives of our Government, military and civilian, who were sent to assist the Chinese in prosecuting the war soon discovered that . . . the long struggle had seriously weakened the Chinese Government not only militarily and economically, but also politically and in morale. The reports of United States military and diplomatic officers reveal a growing conviction through 1943 and 1944 that the Government and the Kuomintang had apparently lost the crusading spirit that won them the people's loyalty during the early years of the war. In the opinion of many observers they had sunk into corruption, into a scramble for place and power, and into reliance on the United States to win the war for them and to preserve their own domestic supremacy. The Government of China, of course, had always been a one-party rather than a democratic government in the Western sense. The stresses and strains of war were now rapidly weakening such liberal elements as it did possess and strengthening the grip of the reactionaries who were indistinguishable from the war lords of the past. The mass of the Chinese people were coming more and more to lose confidence in the Government.

It was evident to us that only a rejuvenated and progressive Chinese Government which could recapture the enthusiastic loyalty of the people could and would wage an effective war against Japan. American officials repeatedly brought their concern with this situation to the attention of the Generalissimo and he repeatedly assured them that it would be corrected. He made, however, little or no effective effort to correct it and tended to shut himself off from Chinese officials who gave unpalatable advice. In addition to a concern over the effect which this atrophy of the central Chinese administration must have upon the conduct of the war, some American observers . . . were concerned over the effect which this deterioration of the Kuomintang must have on its eventual struggle, whether political or military, with the Chinese Communists. These observers were already fearful in 1943 and 1944 that the National Government might be so isolating itself from the people that in the postwar competition for power it would prove itself impotent to maintain its authority. Nevertheless, we continued for obvious reasons to direct all our aid to the National Government.

This was of course the period during which joint prosecution of the war against Nazi Germany had produced a degree of cooperation between the United States and Russia. President Roosevelt was determined to do what he could to bring about a continuance in the postwar period of the partnership forged in the fire of battle. The peoples of the world, sickened and weary with the excesses, the horrors, and the degradation of the war, shared this desire. It has remained for the postwar years to demonstrate that one of the major partners in this world alliance seemingly no longer pursues this aim, if indeed it ever did.

When Maj. Gen. Patrick J. Hurley was sent by President Roosevelt to Chungking in 1944 he found what he considered to be a willingness on the part of the National Government and the Chinese Communists to lay aside their differences and cooperate in a common effort. Already they had been making sporadic attempts to achieve this result.

Previously and subsequently, General Hurley had been assured by Marshal Stalin that Russia had no intention of recognizing any government in China except the National Government with Chiang Kai-shek as its leader. It may be noted that during the late war years and for a time afterwards Marshal Stalin reiterated these views to American officials. He and Molotov expressed the view that China should look to the United States as the principal possible source of aid. The sentiments expressed by Marshal Stalin were in large part incorporated in the Sino-Soviet treaty of 1945.

From the wartime cooperation with the Soviet Union and from the costly campaigns against the Japanese came the Yalta Agreement. The American Government and people awaited with intense anxiety the assault on the main islands of Japan which it was feared would cost up to a million American casualties before Japan was conquered. The atomic bomb was not then a reality and it seemed impossible that the war in the Far East could be ended without this assault. It thus became a primary concern of the American Government to see to it that the Soviet Union enter the war against Japan at the earliest possible date in order that the Japanese Army in Manchuria might not be returned to the homeland at the critical moment. It was considered vital not only that the Soviet Union enter the war but that she do so before our invasion of Japan, which already had been set for the autumn of 1945.

At Yalta, Marshal Stalin not only agreed to attack Japan within two or three months after V–E Day but limited his "price" with reference to Manchuria substantially to the position which Russia had occupied there prior to 1904. We for our part, in order to obtain this commitment and thus to bring the war to a close with a consequent saving of American, Chinese and other Allied lives, were prepared to and did pay the requisite price. Two facts must not, however, be lost sight of in this connection. First, the Soviet Union when she finally did enter the war against Japan, could in any case have seized all the territories in question and considerably more regardless of what our attitude might have been. Second, the Soviets on their side in the Sino-Soviet Treaty arising from the Yalta Agreement, agreed to give the National Government of China moral and material support and moreover formalized their assurances of noninterference in China's internal affairs. Although the unexpectedly early collapse of Japanese resistance later made some of the provisions of the Yalta Agreement seem unnecessary, in the light of the predicted course of the war at that time they were considered to be not only justified but clearly advantageous. Although dictated by military necessity, the Agreement and the subsequent Sino-Soviet Treaty in fact imposed limitations on the action which Russia would, in any case, have been in a position to take.

For reasons of military security, and for those only, it was considered too dangerous for the United States to consult with the National Government regarding the Yalta Agreement or to communicate its terms at once to Chungking. We were then in the midst of the Pacific War. It was felt that there was grave risk that secret information transmitted to the Nationalist capital at this time would become available to the Japanese almost immediately. Under no circumstances, therefore, would we have been justified in incurring the security risks involved. It was not until June 15, 1945, that General Hurley was authorized to inform Chiang Kai-shek of the Agreement.

In conformity with the Russian agreement at Yalta to sign a treaty of friendship and alliance with Nationalist China, negotiations between the two nations began in Moscow in July 1945. During their course, the United States felt obliged to remind both parties that the purpose of the treaty was to implement the Yalta Agreement — no more, no less — and that some of the Soviet proposals exceeded its provisions. The treaty, which was signed on August 14, 1945, was greeted with general satisfaction both in Nationalist China and in the United States. It was considered that Russia had accepted definite limitations on its activities in China and was committed to withhold all aid from the Chinese Communists. On September 10, however, our embassy in Moscow cautioned against placing undue confidence in the Soviet observance of either the spirit or letter of the treaty. The subsequent conduct of the Soviet Government in Manchuria has amply justified this warning.

When peace came the United States was confronted with three possible alternatives in China: (1) it could have pulled out lock, stock and barrel; (2) it could have intervened militarily on a major scale to assist the Nationalists to destroy the Communists; (3) it could, while assisting the Nationalists to assert their authority over as much of China as possible, endeavor to avoid a civil war by working for a compromise between the two sides.[1]

The first alternative would, and I believe American public opinion at the time so felt, have represented an abandonment

---

[1] John S. Service stated the same policy alternatives in his memorandum of June 20, 1944. [Editor's note.]

of our international responsibilities and of our traditional policy of friendship for China before we had made a determined effort to be of assistance. The second alternative policy, while it may look attractive theoretically and in retrospect, was wholly impracticable. The Nationalists had been unable to destroy the Communists during the 10 years before the war. Now after the war the Nationalists were, as indicated above, weakened, demoralized, and unpopular. They had quickly dissipated their popular support and prestige in the areas liberated from the Japanese by the conduct of their civil and military officials. The Communists on the other hand were much stronger than they had ever been and were in control of most of North China. Because of the ineffectiveness of the Nationalist forces which was later to be tragically demonstrated, the Communists probably could have been dislodged only by American arms. It is obvious that the American people would not have sanctioned such a colossal commitment of our armies in 1945 or later. We therefore came to the third alternative policy whereunder we faced the facts of the situation and attempted to assist in working out a *modus vivendi* which would avert civil war but nevertheless preserve and even increase the influence of the National Government.

As the record shows, it was the Chinese National Government itself which, prior to General Hurley's mission, had taken steps to arrive at a working agreement with the Communists. As early as September 1943 in addressing the Kuomintang Central Executive Committee, the Generalissimo said, "we should clearly recognize that the Communist problem is a purely political problem and should be solved by political means." He repeated this view on several occasions. Comprehensive negotiations between representatives of the Government and of the Communists, dealing with both military cooperation and civil administration, were opened in Sian in May 1944. These negotiations, in which Ambassador Hurley later assisted at the invitation of both parties between August 1944 and September 1945, continued intermittently during a year and a half without producing conclusive results and culminated in a comprehensive series of agreements on basic points on October 11, 1945, after Ambassador Hurley's departure from China and before General Marshall's arrival. Meanwhile, however, clashes between the armed forces of the two groups were increasing and were jeopardizing the fulfillment of the agreements. The danger of wide-spread civil war, unless the negotiations could promptly be brought to a successful conclusion, was critical. It was under these circumstances that General Marshall left on his mission to China at the end of 1945.

As the account of General Marshall's mission and the subsequent years . . . reveals, our policy at that time was inspired by the two objectives of bringing peace to China under conditions which would permit stable government and progress along democratic lines, and of assisting the National Government to establish its authority over as wide areas of China as possible. As the event proved, the first objective was unrealizable because neither side desired it to succeed: the Communists because they refused to accept conditions which would weaken their freedom to proceed with what remained consistently their aim, the communization of all China; the Nationalists because they cherished the illusion, in spite of repeated advice to the contrary from our military representatives, that they could destroy the Communists by force of arms.

The second objective of assisting the National Government, however, we pursued vigorously from 1945 to 1949. . . . The National Government had in 1945, and maintained until the early fall of 1948, a marked superiority in manpower and armament over their rivals. Indeed during that period, thanks very largely to our aid in transporting, arming and supplying their forces, they extended their control over a large part of North China and Manchuria.

By the time General Marshall left China at the beginning of 1947, the Nationalists were apparently at the very peak of their military successes and territorial expansion. The following year and a half revealed, however, that their seeming strength was illusory and that their victories were built on sand.

The crisis had developed around Manchuria, traditional focus of Russian and Japanese imperialism. On numerous occasions, Marshal Stalin had stated categorically that he expected the National Government to take over the occupation of Manchuria. In the truce agreement of January 10, 1946, the Chinese Communists agreed to the movement of Government troops into Manchuria for the purpose of restoring Chinese sovereignty over this area. In conformity with this understanding the United States transported sizable government armies to the ports of entry into Manchuria. Earlier the Soviet Army had expressed a desire to evacuate Manchuria in December 1945, but had remained an additional two or three months at the request of the Chinese Government. When the Russian troops did begin their evacuation, the National Government found itself with extended lines of communications, limited rolling stock and insufficient forces to take over the areas being evacuated in time to prevent the entry of Chinese Communist forces, who were already in occupation of the countryside. As the Communists entered, they obtained the large stocks of matériel from the Japanese Kwantung Army which the Russians had conveniently "abandoned." To meet this situation the National Government embarked on a series of military campaigns which expanded the line of its holdings to the Sungari River. Toward the end of these campaigns it also commenced hostilities within North China and succeeded in constricting the areas held by the Communists.

In the spring of 1946 General Marshall attempted to restore peace. This effort lasted for months and during its course a seemingly endless series of proposals and counterproposals were made which had little effect upon the course of military activities and produced no political settlement. During these negotiations General Marshall displayed limitless patience and tact and a willingness to try and then try again in order to reach agreement. Increasingly he became convinced, however, that twenty years of intermittent civil war between the two factions, during which the leading figures had remained the same, had created such deep personal bitterness and such irreconcilable differences that no agreement was possible. The suspicions and the lack of confidence were beyond remedy. He became convinced that both parties were merely sparring for time, jockeying for military position and catering temporarily to what they believed to be American desires. General Marshall concluded that there was no hope of accomplishing the objectives of his mission.

Even though for all practical purposes General Marshall, by the fall of 1946, had withdrawn from his efforts to assist in a peaceful settlement of the civil war, he remained in China until January 1947. One of the critical points of dispute between the Government and the Communists had been the convocation of the National Assembly to write a new constitution for China and to bring an end to the period of political tutelage and of one-party government. The Communists had refused to participate in the National Assembly unless there were a prior military settlement. The Generalissimo was determined that the Assembly should be held and the program carried out. It was the hope of General Marshall during the late months of 1946 that his presence in China would encourage the liberal elements in non-Communist China to assert themselves more forcefully than they had in the past and to exercise a leavening influence upon the absolutist control wielded by the reactionaries and the militarists. General Marshall remained in China until the Assembly had completed its work. Even though the proposed new framework of government appeared satisfactory, the evidence suggested that there had been little shift in the balance of power.

In his farewell statement, General Marshall announced the termination of his efforts to assist the Chinese in restoring internal peace. He described the deep-seated mutual suspicion between the Kuomintang and the Chinese Communist Party as the greatest obstacle to a settlement. He made it clear that the salvation of China lay in the hands of the Chinese themselves and that, while the newly adopted constitution provided the framework for a democratic China, practical measures of implementation by both sides would be the decisive test. He appealed for the assumption of leadership by liberals in and out of the Government as the road to unity and peace. With these final words he returned to Washington to assume, in January 1947, his new post as Secretary of State.

As the signs of impending disaster multiplied, the President in July 1947, acting on the recommendation of the Secretary of State, instructed Lt. Gen. Albert C. Wedemeyer to survey the Chinese scene and make recommendations. In his report, submitted on September 19, 1947, the General recommended that the United States continue and expand its policy of giving aid to Nationalist China, subject to these stipulations:

1. That China inform the United Nations of her request for aid.

2. That China request the United Nations to bring about a truce in Manchuria and request that Manchuria be placed under a Five-Power guardianship or a trusteeship.

3. That China utilize her own resources, reform her finances, her Government and her armies, and accept American advisers in the military and economic fields.

General Wedemeyer's report, which fully recognized the danger of Communist domination of all China and was sympathetic to the problems of the National Government, nevertheless listed a large number of reforms which he considered essential if that Government were to rehabilitate itself.

It was decided that the publication at that time of a suggestion for the alienation of a part of China from the control of the National Government, and for placing that part under an international administration to include Soviet Russia, would not be helpful. . . .

The reasons for the failures of the Chinese National Government . . . do not stem from any inadequacy of American aid. Our military observers on the spot have reported that the Nationalist armies did not lose a single battle during the crucial year of 1948 through lack of arms or ammunition.[2] The fact was that the decay which our observers had detected in Chungking early in the war had fatally sapped the powers of resistance of the Kuomintang. Its leaders had proved incapable of meeting the crisis confronting them, its troops had lost the will to fight, and its Government had lost popular support. The Communists, on the other hand, through a ruthless discipline and fanatical zeal, attempted to sell themselves as guardians and liberators of the people. The Nationalist armies did not have to be defeated; they disintegrated. History has proved again and again that a regime without faith in itself and an army without morale cannot survive the test of battle.

Fully recognizing that the heads of the Chinese Communist Party were ideologically affiliated with Moscow, our Government nevertheless took the view, in the light of the existing balance of forces in China, that peace could be established only if certain conditions were met. The Kuomintang would have to set its own house in order and both sides would have to make concessions so that the Government of China might become, in fact as well as in name, the Government of all China and

---

[2] Major General David Barr, Director of the Joint United States Military Advisory Group to China, so reported in early 1949. [Editor's note.]

so that all parties might function within the constitutional system of the Government. Both internal peace and constitutional development required that the progress should be rapid from one-party government with a large opposition party in armed rebellion, to the participation of all parties, including the moderate non-communist elements, in a truly national system of government.

None of these conditions has been realized. The distrust of the leaders of both the Nationalist and Communist Parties for each other proved too deep-seated to permit final agreement, notwithstanding temporary truces and apparently promising negotiations. The Nationalists, furthermore, embarked in 1946 on an over-ambitious military campaign in the face of warnings by General Marshall that it not only would fail but would plunge China into economic chaos and eventually destroy the National Government. General Marshall pointed out that though Nationalist armies could, for a period, capture Communist-held cities, they could not destroy the Communist armies. Thus every Nationalist advance would expose their communications to attack by Communist guerrillas and compel them to retreat or to surrender their armies together with the munitions which the United States has furnished them. No estimate of a military situation has ever been more completely confirmed by the resulting facts.

The historic policy of the United States of friendship and aid toward the people of China was, however, maintained in both peace and war. Since V–J Day, the United States Government has authorized aid to Nationalist China in the form of grants and credits totaling approximately 2 billion dollars, an amount equivalent in value to more than 50 percent of the monetary expenditures of the Chinese Government and of proportionately greater magnitude in relation to the budget of that Government than the United States has provided to any nation of Western Europe since the end of the war. In addition to these grants and credits, the United States Government has sold the Chinese Government large quantities of military and civilian war surplus property with a total procurement cost of over 1 billion dollars, for which the agreed realization to the United States was 232 million dollars. A large proportion of the military supplies furnished the Chinese armies by the United States since V–J Day has, however, fallen into the hands of the Chinese Communists through the military ineptitude of the Nationalist leaders, their defections and surrenders, and the absence among their forces of the will to fight.

It has been urged that relatively small amounts of additional aid — military and economic — to the National Government would have enabled it to destroy Communism in China. The most trustworthy military, economic, and political information available to our Government does not bear out this view.

A realistic appraisal of conditions in China, past and present, leads to the conclusion that the only alternative open to the United States was full-scale intervention in behalf of a Government which had lost the confidence of its own troops and its own people. Such intervention would have required the expenditure of even greater sums than have been fruitlessly spent thus far, the command of Nationalist armies by American officers, and the probable participation of American armed forces — land, sea, and air — in the resulting war. Intervention of such a scope and magnitude would have been resented by the mass of the Chinese people, would have diametrically reversed our historic policy, and would have been condemned by the American people.

It must be admitted frankly that the American policy of assisting the Chinese people in resisting domination by any foreign power or powers is now confronted with the gravest difficulties. The heart of China is in Communist hands. The Communist leaders have foresworn their Chinese heritage and have publicly announced their subservience to a foreign power, Russia, which during the last 50 years, under czars and Communists alike, has been most assiduous in its efforts to extend its control in the Far East. In the recent past, attempts at foreign domination have appeared quite clearly to the Chinese people as external aggression and as such have been bitterly and in the long run successfully resisted. Our aid and encouragement have helped them to resist. In this case, however, the foreign domination has been masked behind the façade of a vast crusading movement which apparently has seemed to many Chinese to be wholly indigenous and national. Under these circumstances, our aid has been unavailing.

The unfortunate but inescapable fact is that the ominous result of the civil war in China was beyond the control of the government of the United States. Nothing that this country did or could have done within the reasonable limits of its capabilities could have changed that result; nothing that was left undone by this country has contributed to it. It was the product of internal Chinese forces, forces which this country tried to influence but could not. A decision was arrived at within China, if only a decision by default.

And now it is abundantly clear that we must face the situation as it exists in fact. We will not help the Chinese or ourselves by basing our policy on wishful thinking. We continue to believe that, however tragic may be the immediate future of China and however ruthlessly a major portion of this great people may be exploited by a party in the interest of a foreign imperialism, ultimately the profound civilization and the democratic individualism of China will reassert themselves and she will throw off the foreign yoke. I consider that we should encourage all developments in China which now and in the future work toward this end.

In the immediate future, however, the implementation of our historic policy of friendship for China must be profoundly affected by current developments. It will necessarily be influenced by the degree to which the Chinese people come to recognize that the Communist regime serves not their interests but those of Soviet Russia and the manner in which, having become aware of the facts, they react to this foreign domination. One point, however, is clear. Should the Communist regime lend itself to the aims of Soviet Russian imperialism and attempt to engage in aggression against China's neighbors, we and the other members of the United Nations would be confronted by a situation violative of the principles of the United Nations Charter and threatening international peace and security.

Meanwhile our policy will continue to be based upon our own respect for the Charter, our friendship for China, and our traditional support for the Open Door and for China's independence and administrative and territorial integrity.

Respectfully yours,

DEAN ACHESON

Communist Designs and Kuomintang Blunders

CHIANG KAI-SHEK

To Chiang Kai-shek (1887–   ), whose political career has been inseparable from the history of the Kuomintang government since the days of the
Northern Expedition of 1926–28, the struggle against the Chinese Communists
has always taken on another dimension: it is a struggle against communism
as a morally perverted materialistic philosophy. In this personal account of
what went awry with his government, he accuses the Soviet Union of plans of
aggression against China, and castigates the Chinese Communists and Democratic Leaguers for having been willing tools of Soviet imperialism. He absolves
the U. S. of primary responsibilities in his government's downfall, although he
makes it amply clear that the Chinese conflict was in more ways than one
"an international and diplomatic problem" and that China's peace and prosperity "depended on whether the American Government could stop the Chinese
Communists' intrigue against the Government."

Suggesting that the war against communism in China does not have to
fail, he identifies his failure as being the result of Kuomintang blunders in
policy and technique, not in objective, due chiefly to an underestimation of
Communist strength, skill, and resilience. This error in judgment, he says, has
influenced his government to accept the Yalta Agreement as an integral part
of the Sino-Soviet Treaty of 1945 and to counter the unlimited war of the
Chinese Communists with limited war. Instead of regarding the Communists
as workable partners, the Kuomintang should have refrained from diplomatic
rapprochement with the Soviet Union in 1932 or from the truce negotiations
with the Chinese communists after 1945, particularly in regard to the highly
sensitive area of Manchuria. In short, there should have been a total separation
of the bad from the good. But above all, Chiang suggests, the Kuomintang
failed because its "spiritual strength" — meaning non-material strength, including will and belief — was not, in the face of the Communist propaganda
of defeatism, equal to the task of national reconstruction.

DURING the Sino-Japanese War the crosscurrent of Communism was held down by the spirit of nationalism, and also by the strict precautions of the Government, with the result that the Chinese Communists' plot to turn a national war into a class war and an external war into an internal war was foiled. Yet, after the war, Soviet Russia and the Chinese Communists succeeded in carrying out their plans of aggression and we met with tragic reverses in our military campaign against the Communist insurrection. Why?

I propose now to analyze the defects in our organization and in our technique as well as mistakes in our policy and in our strategy that were responsible for our defeat.

First of all I must point out that China depended more on spiritual strength than on material strength in her war with Japan. It was this force of national spirit which enabled China to keep on fighting without falter for fourteen years (1931–1945).

The Chinese Government decided, at the outbreak of major hostilities in 1937,

Reprinted from *Soviet Russia in China: A Summing-Up at Seventy* by Chiang Kai-shek, pp.
211–34 by permission of Farrar, Straus & Giroux, Inc. Copyright © 1957 by Farrar, Straus and
Cudahy, Inc.

that it would be a prolonged war and also foresaw that Soviet Russia would take advantage of China's exhaustion at the end of the war to perpetrate her scheme of external aggression and internal subversion against China. For this reason, we formulated the Program of War of Resistance and National Reconstruction in 1938 to strengthen our spiritual mobilization during the war, to carry on national reconstruction and simultaneously to pave the ground for building up China into a modern and strong country with a rising standard of living. Of course, both the Russian and the Chinese Communists also saw this point. That was why, during the war, they coordinated their moves with the Japanese militarists against the Government troops.

When the war ended the Communists resorted to armed insurrection. They did everything to nullify all reconstruction projects, to hinder the Government's program of demobilization, to disrupt the nation's economic life and to upset its social order. They spread national defeatism at a time when the people were weary after the long war. Finally the general public became so confused and bewildered that all that they asked was peace at any cost, however transient it might turn out to be. This was the basic reason for the tragic reverses which China suffered in her war against Communism.

ORGANIZATIONAL AND TECHNICAL DEFECTS
IN OUR STRUGGLE AGAINST COMMUNISM

The first defect in our fight against Communism was that our organization was not strict enough and our vigilance not heightened enough.

It has been the Chinese people's philosophy of life "to conceal others' evils but to extol their virtues," and "not to bear grudges because of past injustices." Kuomintang was built on the basis of China's traditional ethics and national consciousness. This was how we felt toward Chinese Communists both after we took them into our Party in 1924 and after we allowed them to make common cause with the rest

of the nation against Japan in 1937. This was also our attitude toward Soviet Russia after we resumed diplomatic relations with her in 193[2].

In our dealings with the Chinese Communists we have always set a great store by ethical considerations, good faith and righteousness. It was our belief that every Chinese cannot help feeling loyal to his own country first. That was why we had sincerely hoped to move forward together with the Communists on the road of democracy to complete our task of national reconstruction.

What we did not realize was that Communists are Communists, first, last and always. They were traitorous and treacherous all the time. Everywhere they went they set traps for others. Any weak spot in our organization or a loophole in our precautionary measures would give them a chance to start trouble. In our war against Communism we made the mistake of judging the Communists by the same yardstick of national consciousness and democratic and ethical concepts.

For instance, we should have regarded the Communist Party as an illegal body and isolated it so that it could not operate openly. After our Party purge of 1927 we broke off diplomatic relations with Soviet Russia. Throughout the years, the Government steadily refused to accord the Communists a legal status. This was a fundamental way of preventing them from inciting the masses through propaganda. In 1937, however, we made the mistake of acceding to their request for cease-fire and surrender, and of lifting in part the previous ban on their freedoms of propaganda and organization. This political and social loophole gave the Communists an opportunity for infiltration, concealment and expansion.

Both in 1924 and 1936 our Party was in a serious predicament on account of vacillations and internal dissensions. Our greatest mistake lay in the fact that we were not rigid enough in our organization and not heightened enough in our vigilance. Contradictions in our policy furnished the Communists with a schism which they exploited to their advantage.

Then, we should have prevented the Communists from effecting political and social changes. Over a period of thirty years the Communists made common cause with the National Revolution only to sabotage it, and joined the Northward Expedition only to disrupt it. The tactic they used was "to convert a democratic revolution into a social revolution," and "to convert a foreign war into a civil war." We not only saw this tactic in operation but actually experienced it. Of course, we understood it for what it was and took precautions against it.

The people in general, even including some members of our Party and those who had fought Communism for a long time, failed to understand the Communist tactics and, as a result, let up in their vigilance. In some extreme cases they even echoed what others were saying, branding our anti-Communist organizations and propaganda as undemocratic, censuring our anti-Communist measures and laws and orders as opposed to freedom. On the contrary, they came to mistake the Communists' "New Democracy" for genuine democratic ideas, their "United Front" for a democratic movement and their "Coalition Government" as democracy itself. Little did they know that all these were but the application in China of the methods by which Moscow had conquered the Eastern European countries. According to Moscow's formula, what the Chinese Communists called "New Democracy," "United Front" and "Coalition Government" were but combat slogans which the Chinese Communists had devised in accordance with their dialectic law of negation for subversive purposes.

Once the Communists seized political power they changed the country qualitatively first into a "people's democratic dictatorship" and then into a "socialist state," which, in fact, is nothing but a Soviet satellite. Their final aim was to push the Chinese mainland into Soviet Russia's Red orbit. This is plain enough today, but, at the time, most people were ignorant of the real nature of Communism, and their lack of vigilance enabled the Communists to perpetrate their intrigues and inflict on the Chinese mainland this unprecedented catastrophe. This was the greatest defect in our struggle against Communism.

Secondly, we lacked initiative in propaganda and substance in ideology.

Whenever the Chinese Communists met with reverses in the field, international Communists came to their rescue by spreading propaganda aimed at confusing the general public as well as people in the Government. This happened at the time of our Party purge in 1927, our successful military campaign against the Communist rebels in 1935 and again at the end of the war in 1945.

By comparison, our propaganda lacked initiative and was not militant enough in ideology to counter this international political and psychological offensive, nor was it strong enough to arouse indignation at home and a sense of righteousness abroad. In consequence, our Government was beset with difficulties both internally and internationally. Although several times we fought, we vacillated and did not press on all the way through.

The first point which the Communists used in their propaganda was "Opposition to Communism is Fascism." After World War I there were two crosscurrents. These were Communism in Soviet Russia, and Fascism in Germany, Italy and Japan. Both were antidemocratic totalitarianisms, and as such both were enemies of democracy. After the seventh congress of the Communist International in 1935 Communists in various countries were directed to form "United Fronts" with Socialists, and even with democratic parties, to oppose Fascism. Through the propaganda and rabble-rousing of Communists and their fellow travelers, the democratic nations developed a fear of Fascism. In the meantime there had come into circulation a "pseudo logic" which said "Opposition to Communism is Fascism." This finally forced us to hold peace talks and political consultations with the Chinese Communists. Our failure in propaganda was a major defect in our struggle against Communism.

Whenever the Chinese Communists were faced with defeat and destruction, they also paraded the theory that "the Communist Party is destructible, but not Communism."

Both after our successful military drive against the Communists in 1935 and after victory in 1945 we failed to counter this Communist theory, which in the end gained considerable credence. This not only saved the Communists from destruction, but also shook the people's confidence in their ability to liquidate the Chinese Communists.

The Communists also contended that "the Communist problem cannot be solved by military means and, therefore, it must be settled by political means." This point was made much use of by international Communists and their Chinese puppets in their propaganda at the end of our war with Japan. They argued that military force could only annihilate the Communist forces, but not solve the problem of the Communist Party. They alleged that if the Government should try to settle the Communist troops by force of arms, it would cause national bankruptcy, wreak untold hardships on the people, enable Communism and Communist organizations to spread and that the Government would wind up as the real loser. So the people, both in China and abroad, came to think that "fighting the Communists is tantamount to manufacturing Communists," and they used this slogan to oppose the Government's policy of suppressing the Communist rebellion by force. Again, our propaganda failed to counter this political and psychological offensive. Thus the only way open to the Government was to hold peace talks and to convene the Political Consultative Conference.

In reality what Moscow has laid down,

and what the Chinese Communists have been faithfully following as a creed, is that "a peculiarity with the Chinese Revolution is the use of revolutionary arms against counterrevolutionary arms." This is to say that the Chinese Communists, in their struggle for power, must use force against the Government. The Chinese Communists feared that the moment they gave up their arms they would forfeit their very existence. In order to solve the Communist problem and to liquidate the Communist troops, therefore, it was essential for us to use both military and political strength to defeat their armed forces and also their political organization.

At the end of the Sino-Japanese War the contention that "the Communist problem can only be solved by political means and, therefore, it must not be settled by military means" led the people to the erroneous belief that a political solution was the only way out for the Government. This shook even the confidence of people in the Government's ability to suppress the Communists by force. Finally the Government had to yield and to agree to hold political consultation and peace talks with the Communists. This created a state of affairs when there was neither war nor peace, and when there were both fighting and peace talks.

Moreover, we failed to fortify our will against Communism and also failed to take drastic actions. Soviet Russia and its tool of aggression, the international Communists, always aim at either domination or destruction. The fate they have in store for the masses is either enslavement or oppression. All such things as united front, neutralism, peace talks, political consultation and even terms and agreements written in black and white are merely forms of struggle which they happen to use at the time. For the final showdown they will invariably resort to violence. They are ruthless in actions and treacherous in methods. If you do not destroy them, they will eventually destroy you. In our efforts to solve the Communist problem and to liquidate the Communist armed forces, often because of domestic and foreign obstacles, we were not sufficiently thorough in our actions. Thus we met with defeat.

First, we made the mistake of countering the Communists' unlimited war with limited war. The successful conclusion of the Government's fifth military drive against the Communists in 1935 was made possible by combining all our political, economic, social and military strength. In 1947 the situation was vastly different. By then the Communists had infiltrated the Government and defeatism was prevalent throughout the country. There were impediments to mobilization, chaos in schools, social instability, inflation and other financial difficulties. To make matters worse the Government was subjected to hostile international propaganda and the pressure of intrigues. The morale of both the armed forces and the civilian population was at a low ebb. Only the armed forces fought, and even they felt the effect of defeatism. In waging limited war against the Communists' total war, the Government was predestined to failure.

Secondly, we underestimated the Communists' capacity and capability for brutality and violence. China is a big country and has had a long history and a superior culture. Its people are traditionally peace-loving and have the highest respect for good faith and righteousness. Under Dr. Sun's guidance, the people have developed a strong faith in the Three People's Principles, and supported the cause of the National Revolution. Despite vicissitudes and setbacks, Dr. Sun held tenaciously to the belief that our efforts in revolution and national reconstruction would result in success. I share the same belief.

As explained earlier, Soviet Russia's Communism is not suitable to our national spirit and culture. The reign of terror which the Chinese Communists perpetrated in class struggle was opposed to our ethical concepts. As early as 1923 Dr. Sun and Joffe affirmed in their joint declaration that Communism cannot be applied to China. After admitting the Chinese Communists into Kuomintang, Dr. Sun was struck by the underhand methods used by Chen Tu-hsiu, leader of the Chinese Communist Party, and others with dual-party memberships, but he still thought that they could not cause China any harm. Though I became anti-Communist as a result of my visit to Soviet Russia, I was overconfident too, and failed to settle the Communist problem in a fundamental manner.

I have shown that in the years between our Party purge in 1927 and our successful military drive in 1935, our policy toward the Communists remained one of suppression short of annihilation. Whenever the Communists' military force was crushed and their political organization smashed, we tried to appeal to their national consciousness in the hope that they would mend their ways and work for the country. That was why we did not pursue the Communist remnants in their flight to the Northwest, and, later, even acceded to their request for truce and surrender.

In 1936 there were less than 5,000 men in their army when the Communists were bottled up in northern Shensi. With the Japanese war of aggression drawing increasingly near, the Government did not harass them further, but instead agreed to discuss a political settlement with them. During the war the Government cordoned off the Communist area to prevent them from establishing a direct line of communication with Soviet Russia through the Northwest.

At the same time the Government held five series of discussions with the Chinese Communists, hoping against hope that the latter, no matter how treacherous they might have been, would eventually yield to the pressure of patriotism and public opinion.

When the war ended the country was in need of rehabilitation and reconstruction, and the people were all looking forward to demobilization. As the unequal treaties had already been abolished, the nation felt a new sense of independence. Any Chinese with a national consciousness would feel loyal to the country and refrain from engaging in any traitorous activities against the nation. Consequently, the Government decided upon a program of peaceful reconstruction and accepted American mediation in its negotiations with the Communists. Today, looking back at the situation, we realize we were overconfident and failed sufficiently to take into account the Communists' brutalities and violence imbedded in their class nature and international character. We erred in being too lenient with them. This gave them a chance to perpetrate their political intrigues which ended in bringing on this unprecedented calamity to our people.

Moreover, though we took precautions against the Chinese Communists, we neglected their front organizations. These appear in various forms to serve various purposes. Whenever the Communist Party is outlawed, and hence cannot openly engage in activities, it directs leftist elements and fellow travelers to carry on such activities on its behalf. Even when the Communist Party does have a legal status and can be active in the open, it uses the leftist elements in making flank or envelopment attacks.

One of the mistakes which we made in our struggle against Communism, and which becomes perfectly clear today, is that we were not as strict in our preventive measures against the Communist Party as against the Communist armed forces, and we did not pay as much attention to the leftists and neutralists in the Communist front as to the Communist Party itself. For that reason, although we defeated the Communist armed forces repeatedly in the field, we did not destroy the Communists' organization. In other words, we succeeded in annihilating the visible Communist Party, but failed to checkmate the activities of the invisible Communist front. In reality, so long as the leftist elements and the neutralist bodies could carry on with their activities, the Communists would be able to conceal themselves. It follows that so long as the front organizations could expand, the Communists would always have a base for their armed uprising. That was why the Communists and their armed forces, despite their repeated defeats at the hands of Government forces between 1927 and 1935, were able to stay alive and to stage a comeback at a later date.

Then, too, our people's morale, which reached its height during the Sino-Japanese War, suffered a setback because of Communist propaganda. This also affected our spiritual mobilization.

It should be remembered that China had lived under unequal treaties for a century, and consequently most of the people needed to restore their sense of national self-respect and self-confidence. In our National Revolution to save the country, we made psychological reconstruction our first task. The New Life Movement, which was started after the Japanese attack on Mukden, was in reality an organized effort at reviving national self-confidence through changing the people's way of life. Then during the war we launched the Spiritual Mobilization Movement to stimulate the growth of national spirit in order to accelerate mobilization in other phases of our national life. Upon the abolition of unequal treaties at the end of the war, China's national equality and freedom were assured. We had a wonderful opportunity for reconstruction. At this juncture the Chinese Communists and their front organizations spread defeatism while international Communists launched a smearing campaign against our country and our Government. All our efforts at psychological reconstruction were thus nullified. Finally, the people lost their will to fight Communism, and the Government's policy of putting down the insurrection by force, backed by a partial mobilization, ended in failure.

Two other factors leading to the disaster on the mainland were diplomatic isolation and economic collapse caused by malignant inflation.

From behind the Iron Curtain Soviet

Russia directs the international Communists in the various nations in collecting intelligence, inciting the masses, manipulating public opinion, creating pressure and subverting the policies of the governments concerned. Meanwhile the Chinese society is free and open, and our country is still new to institutionalized democracy. In dealing with Soviet Russia, we found ourselves in a disadvantageous position. In fact, even in coping with the problem posed by the Chinese Communists, we found it difficult to win international sympathy and help. In the end, we were completely isolated. Consider a few instances:

We tried to counter the Russian Communists' treachery with good faith and sincerity, and consequently were put on the defensive in our negotiations with Soviet Russia. During the thirty years under review China and Soviet Russia had concluded the Sino-Soviet Agreement of 1924, the Non-Aggression Pact of 1937 and the Treaty of Friendship and Alliance of 1945. We voluntarily adhered to every one of these agreements both in letter and in spirit, and used them as the basis for our negotiations. To the Russian Communists these agreements were just so many pieces of paper which they could sign and tear up at will.

The most infamous example of Soviet Russia's bad faith was in her obstructing the Chinese Government troops from moving into Manchuria at the end of World War II to re-establish Chinese authority there in accordance with stipulations in the Sino-Soviet Treaty of Friendship and Alliance and in her turning the territory into a base for rearming the Chinese Communists and setting them against the Government.

In dealing with the problem on Manchuria our Government was bound by the Sino-Soviet Treaty and restricted by American mediation. This was our reward for meeting the Russian Communists' treachery with good faith and sincerity.

Again, we and our allies tried to counter the over-all intrigues of the Soviet bloc severally and without unity. Soviet Russia decided upon her postwar world policy in 1943 and picked China as the first target. If the free nations had coordinated their moves at the end of World War II, and had reached an understanding concerning Soviet Russia, our Government would have been able to keep the situation at home under control, check Communist expansion and safeguard national security as our contribution toward the maintenance of peace in Asia and in the world.

Of course, the men in the Kremlin knew this. That was why they ordered the international Communists to discredit our Government both in world public opinion and in diplomacy before they defeated our forces in the military field. To alienate Sino-American cooperation, Stalin tried neutralism tactics on our Government to ensure China's neutrality. At the same time, during the Marshall mission, he used the same tactic to make the United States adopt a neutral policy toward China. It was under this pressure that the United States evacuated her troops from China, and also ceased her financial and military assistance to my country. Pro-Communists in the United States used all the slanderous attacks suggested by Soviet Russia against our Government, and against me personally. This meant that the Chinese Government, besides facing the enemy's pressure at home, was subjected to international pressure as well. This caused China's isolation. The free world, including ourselves, brought on this defeat by meeting Soviet Russia's over-all intrigues with divided views and individual efforts.

On the eve of our victory my Government and my people were all optimistic about postwar reconstruction. No sooner was the war over than plans were laid for military demobilization and civilian rehabilitation. The pressure of inflation at the end of the long war was mounting daily. This was all the more reason for the people's anxiousness for demobilization and economic reconstruction. If this had been smoothly carried out the problem of malignant inflation could have been solved. The Communists, however, did everything possible to sabotage the Government's economic policies and made it necessary for the Government to combat them in the economic field as well as in the military and political fields.

In defending itself against Communist economic warfare the Government had to exert itself both in domestic affairs and in foreign relations. Internally, the Government had difficulty in balancing its budget, the main reason being the excessively large military expenditure. In order to cut down expenses for the armed forces it had to reduce the latter's size. The Communists were fully aware of this point and did their best to defeat the American mediation effort in order to prevent the Government from carrying out its plans for military reorganization and demobilization. Meanwhile, for the sake of restoring law and order disrupted by the Communists, the Government had to mobilize again, this time to put down an open rebellion.

Meanwhile, it was the Government's policy to welcome foreign capital and technical cooperation on a basis of equality and mutual benefit to develop our economy and build up our industries for the purpose of raising the people's standard of living. On the other hand, it was part of Moscow's plan of aggression against China to isolate our Government and to undermine our national economy and the Chinese people's way of life. The Russian Communists were particularly determined to sabotage Sino-American economic cooperation so as to facilitate their scheme against our Government and our country. This economic war by the Russian Communists was directed not only against China but against the United States as well. On the one hand, they instigated the Chinese Communists to interfere with the Government's reconstruction plans by cutting communications and damaging factories and mines in various parts of the country. On the other, they ordered the American Communists and their fellow travelers to create sentiments, both in the press and in the diplomatic field, against the conclusion of a loan by the American Government to China, and also against investments in China by the American people.

The effectiveness of this economic war was proved by the sudden halt in the consummation of the US$500,000,000 credit loan which had already been agreed upon.[1] This came at the time of the Political Consultative Conference and American mediation in the military field. It was the American Government's intention to bring pressure to bear on our Government to accept mediation for internal peace. It had apparently thought that this would help us in our postwar reconstruction. From the Chinese Communists' point of view, however, the successful conclusion of the loan would deal a mortal blow to their plot of armed rebellion and political subversion. Consequently they simply had to defeat it.

Meanwhile, as far as the Chinese people in general were concerned, they believed that whether China would have domestic peace or disturbances, economic prosperity or poverty depended on demobilization and reconstruction which, in turn, depended on whether the American Government could stop the Chinese Communists' intrigue against the Government. In other words, if the loan went through as agreed upon, it would be a demonstration of the American Government's determination and sincerity to help the Chinese Government in its effort to restore law and order in the country and to start peaceful reconstruction. This would be the only way to stop the rebellion of the Communists and to foil their subversive schemes.

[1] This is probably a reference to the 500 million dollars which the Import-Export Bank authorized in April 1946, upon the recommendation of General George C. Marshall and with the approval of the National Advisory Council, for the possible extension of credits to the Chinese government and private Chinese interests. No implementing agreements were reached, however, between the Bank and the Chinese Government because, according to a State Department report, "the Bank was unable to find reasonable assurances of repayment regarding which it had a statutory obligation." [Editor's note.]

Unfortunately, once the Chinese Communists made known their opposition the United States postponed the execution of the loan agreement indefinitely. Thus, in a single stroke, the international Communists succeeded in undermining the foundation of Sino-American economic cooperation. The American Government's decision had a tremendous psychological effect on the Chinese people. As a result the people began to lose confidence in the chance of national reconstruction. For the same reason the Government's financial and economic measures failed to achieve their purpose, and its economic planning and implementation met with continuous setbacks. In improvising its actions the Government committed a number of mistakes. For instance, the first postwar Executive Yuan, between September 1945 and February 1947, made use of our currency reform reserve fund in an attempt to cope with financial difficulties and disturbances in the monetary and credit field at the time. This made it impossible for the Government to lay down any concrete and effective policy in general or any long-term currency stabilization plan in particular. The second Executive Yuan issued U. S. dollar bonds in March 1947 but had to discontinue the issuance shortly afterward. The third Executive Yuan's currency reform plan whereby gold dollar certificates were issued in August 1948 resulted in further deterioration of our currency.

The Chinese Communists immediately seized upon this situation and through their malicious propaganda succeeded in confusing the people. To make things worse for the Government, the Communists manipulated the currency and price fluctuation in the various big cities. Soon inflation got out of control. This resulted in widespread demoralization among the civil servants as well as among the armed forces. It was no longer possible to maintain military discipline at the same high level as during the war years. This was one of the main causes for our defeat in fighting the Communists. Regardless of whether this was brought about by our own mistakes or by force of circumstances, it is imperative that we should restudy it analytically and draw lessons of vigilance from it.

ERRORS IN OUR POLICY AND STRATEGY AGAINST COMMUNISM

Above we have noted the four major defects in organization and technique in our war against Communism. These, however, were all remediable. Even if they could not be completely rectified, so long as we remained determined, and so long as our strategy and policy were correct, I believe we still could have won.

Let us analyze the errors in policy and strategy which we have committed in combating Communism in the past.

What was our greatest error in policy in our struggle against Communism? Many thought that our first error was in accepting the terms of the Yalta Agreement and in concluding the Sino-Soviet Treaty of Friendship and Alliance because the secret terms at Yalta bartered away China's territorial sovereignty as a price for Soviet Russia's participation in the war against Japan. It was felt that by accepting these terms and signing the treaty we gave Soviet Russia a legal basis for her aggression in Manchuria and paved the way for the Chinese Communists to bring harm to the country.

We signed the Treaty of Friendship and Alliance with Soviet Russia, however, not because we recognized the Yalta Agreement or because we considered it binding on us. As the Republic of China did not attend the Yalta Conference, and as the United States did not consult us either before or during the Yalta Conference, we were not bound by its decisions. While it is true that we negotiated the treaty with Soviet Russia upon the advice of the United States, we did so after having given the matter our own consideration.

For half a century China, in her effort to win national independence and freedom and to help preserve world peace and security, had been faced with the dual threat of Japanese and Russian aggression. After Japan's surrender in 1945 we needed from twenty to thirty years of peace for reconstruction and it was our hope to be able to find a way to live in peace with Soviet Russia. This was what prompted us to sign the Sino-Soviet Treaty of Friendship and Alliance.

We had considered duly the possibility that Soviet Russia, in view of her record of bad faith, might scuttle the treaty. What could we do in such an eventuality? I had this in mind when I told Kuomintang's Central Standing Committee at the time of the signing of the treaty: "Even if Soviet Russia should continue her policy of aggression against us, this treaty will serve as a yardstick with which the world can judge her actions, and also as a basis on which we can conduct our negotiations." What we did, therefore, cannot be put down *per se* as a great error in our policy.

It was generally thought that our second error was in accepting American mediation in our conflict with the Communists. Of course, the Chinese Communists had their own reasons for accepting it. Why did our Government accept American mediation and conclude the cease-fire agreement to bind its own hands and feet?

The international situation at the time was such that we would become more isolated if we did not sign the Sino-Soviet Treaty and did not accept American mediation. Although our Government was strong enough to dispose of the Chinese Communists, it alone did not have the necessary strength to oppose Soviet imperialism and stop Russian troops from entering Manchuria and from helping the Chinese Communists. The Government had to consider its moral and material resources. For the sake of domestic peace it was ready to do anything that was honorable. In dealing with friends it was utterly sincere. As long as we did our best and remained true to our moral standard, what we did can hardly be called a major error in our policy.

In the opinion of some people, our third error was in instituting constitutional gov-

ernment before we had put down the Communist insurrection. It was said that in the interest of effective prosecution of the war against the Communists the mind of the people should be concentrated and not distracted, and that elections, instead of promoting unity, would accentuate diversity and antagonism in the country. This would not only cause greater divergencies and contradictions between the various political parties but would also have an adverse effect on our party organization and discipline. The Communists, under the cloak of "democracy" and "freedom," took advantage of this situation to step up their infiltration and diverse activities and to spread defeatism. In the end the Government's military effort against the Communists failed.

It should be remembered, however, that the aim of our National Revolution was to build up China as a democratic nation. We had decided at the beginning of the war that the day of victory would also mark the commencement of constitutional government in China. Consequently, shortly after the war ended, our Government decided to convene the National Assembly for the purpose of initiating constitutional rule. I felt at the time that if we should really meet with defeat because of our decision to launch constitutional rule in the country, we should have no cause for regret or remorse. Subsequent events have proved that our efforts in this respect have been a success.

We firmly believe that only democracy and government by law can give us the necessary strength to defeat Communist totalitarianism, and only a democratic constitution can provide a sharp contrast to the reign of terror and brutality which the Chinese Communists have inflicted on the people. Therefore, we committed no serious error in launching constitutional rule before we had put down the Communist insurrection, despite the fact that this step did cause us certain disadvantages in our military effort against the Communists.

Since these three cannot be regarded as

serious factors in our military disaster, what then were our errors in point of policy and strategy? In my opinion, there were four of them.

The first one was the resumption of diplomatic relations with Soviet Russia.

After the Japanese attack on Mukden Moscow was anxious to stop the Japanese advance in the north and, therefore, hoped to resume diplomatic relations with China. The Chinese Government gave this matter its most careful consideration but it was not until December 1932 that an agreement was reached.

For five years (1933–1937), however, there was no progress whatsoever in Sino-Soviet relations. On the contrary, Soviet Russia tried hard to move closer to Japan. This was made abundantly clear in her sale of the Chinese Eastern Railway to the Japanese puppet state of "Manchukuo" despite the fact that it was in violation of China's sovereign rights in Manchuria.

In 1937 China and Soviet Russia concluded a Nonaggression Pact and a barter agreement. Soviet Russia drove hard bargains regarding Chinese exports, and the arms she supplied us were mostly not accompanied by enough spare parts and were not available when they were most needed. This flow of supplies stopped completely in 1941.

In April 1941 Soviet Russia and Japan concluded a Neutrality Pact which encouraged Japanese aggression against the Western powers. This was in violation of the Sino-Soviet Agreement of 1924 and the Sino-Soviet Nonaggression Pact of 1937.

It should be remembered that, once Sino-Soviet diplomatic relations were resumed in 1932, Soviet Russia set up diplomatic, consular and trade missions in China which were used to harbor espionage centers and organs for directing the activities of Chinese Communists against our country. The Russians used the highway in the Northwest to provide a link between Moscow and Yenan. In Shanghai the Soviet consulate not only became the liaison office between Chinese Communists and Japanese secret service organs, but also represented Moscow in giving encouragement and support to the Wang Ching-wei puppet regime. In Tihua the Soviet consulate served as the command post from which all incidents and strifes in Sinkiang province were manipulated.

Thus, it is clear that the resumption of diplomatic relations with Soviet Russia, instead of bringing us any help in the Sino-Japanese War, had actually caused us considerable harm. China lost more than she gained as a result. Our fourteen years of war with Japan (1931–1945) showed how deceptive was the view, widely held at the time, that China could resist Japan only by aligning herself with Soviet Russia. Our Government made an error in policy and in strategy when it resumed diplomatic relations with Soviet Russia.

The reorganization and integration of the Communist troops was also an important factor. In 1934, two years after China had resumed her diplomatic relations with Soviet Russia, the Government launched its final military drive against the Chinese Communists. It proceeded to seek a political settlement of the Communist problem. After the Sino-Japanese War began the Government took steps to integrate the Communist troops into its armed forces. While it is true that we decided upon this policy in the face of the Japanese militarists' threat of invasion, we also overconfidently believed that the Communists' demand for "united resistance to Japan" was an evidence of the rise of China's national spirit and consciousness above everything else. Unfortunately, this belief played into the hands of the Communists, who, as we have seen, took advantage of the war to attack Government troops, to expand their armed forces, to spread defeatism and to subvert the Government in coordination with the Japanese.

So our decision to take in the Communist troops and to permit the Communist Party to join the national war effort against Japan on an equal footing with other political parties was definitely harmful to the nation It was an error both in policy and in strategy for the Government to negotiate with the Communists and to take their troops into the Government forces.

Furthermore, the Government also committed a great error in handling the Manchurian problem.

It may be said that it was China's resumption of diplomatic relations with Soviet [Russia] in 1932 which subsequently led to the latter's entry into the Pacific region. By 1945 and 1946 Soviet Russia's intrigues and bad faith regarding Manchuria became perfectly clear. At first we decided to stop trying to re-establish Chinese authority in the region, but later changed our mind. We continued discussions with her and went on with the take-over operations. This was where we made a serious error in policy and in strategy.

Manchuria is a part of China, its people are Chinese citizens and its resources are *absolutely essential to China's reconstruction*. Our stand on this matter remained firm. Our security in Manchuria, in other words, whether or not it fell into the hands of Russian Communists, was a matter of international concern. Since China alone could not solve the problem, and since it could not be solved by our negotiations with Soviet Russia, we should have called off the take-over operations altogether. Then we could have concentrated our armed forces in the Peiping-Tientsin area, held Shanhaikwan and used Chinchow as a forward base. In the meantime, we could have submitted the Manchurian problem to the United Nations for a decision and held Soviet Russia responsible for all consequences by appealing to world opinion. In this way our Government would have had the necessary military strength below the Great Wall to put down the Communist revolt, control all of North China and use the international deliberations to expose Soviet Russia's designs on Manchuria and her eastward advance to the Pacific.

Owing to domestic and foreign interferences we failed to adhere to our earlier policy. Instead, we held direct negotiations with Soviet Russia. At the same time we made the mistake of committing the best Government troops to Manchuria only to bog down there. Finally Manchuria fell, and the Government had to evacuate North China as well. By that time the entire situation was out of control.

A fourth error in policy and strategy was in connection with the cease-fire agreement.

It may be remembered that the cease-fire agreement was signed in January, 1946. This was followed by the convening of the Political Consultative Conference. Both the Chinese Government and the United States correctly maintained that Manchuria must not be included among the topics for political consultation; Government troops, sent to Manchuria or moving from one place to another in the region to re-establish Chinese authority there, were not to be affected by the cease-fire agreement.

As the Government looked at it, troops sent to Manchuria to re-establish Chinese sovereignty there did not come under the cease-fire agreement especially since Moscow had admitted that there were no Chinese Communist troops there.

Also, the fact that the Government was carrying on negotiations with Soviet Russia for the re-establishment of Chinese sovereignty in Manchuria on the basis of the Sino-Soviet Treaty showed that this was an international and diplomatic problem and not an internal and political problem. For this reason it should not become a topic for political consultation.

Soviet Russia and her Chinese puppets, including the Democratic League, however, sought to turn the question of restoring China's sovereignty in Manchuria into a problem between the Government and the Chinese Communists, and hence a matter fit for military mediation. They even suggested that the United States and Soviet Russia should mediate jointly. The Communists tried to wring from the Government recognition of their illegal actions and of accomplished facts in Manchuria. It was in support of Soviet Russia's intrigue there that the Chinese Communists launched all-out offensives in several North China provinces. This compelled the Marshall mission's Subcommittee of Three to discuss with the Chinese Communists a formula for military mediation in Manchuria. Our Government, however, still refused to let the Manchurian problem be discussed in the Political Consultative Conference or in its General Committee.

The Chinese Communists' main conflict with the Government was actually over Manchuria. Our attitude was that the question of re-establishing Chinese authority in Manchuria could no longer be solved by China and Soviet Russia alone, and that despite Chinese Communist agitation to the contrary, it should not be considered a domestic political problem.

The Chinese Communists tried to use their insurrection south of the Great Wall to make the Government yield in Manchuria. If the Government had concentrated its military forces and taken action against the Communist troops for their violations of the cease-fire agreement of January 1946, even at the risk of provoking an all-out war, it could have won. As to the question of restoring Chinese sovereignty in Manchuria, the Government had earlier decided to submit it to the United Nations so that it would not be confused with military operations below the Great Wall. Unfortunately, we vacillated on this all-important problem and failed to stick to our earlier decision. This brought upon ourselves a catastrophic defeat in the field.

THE DYNAMICS OF CHINESE REVOLUTION

Historical Imperatives and the Chinese Pattern of Rule

CHARLES P. FITZGERALD

Professor Fitzgerald (1902–), whose first sojourn in China dates back to 1923, was British Council Representative in North China and cultural attaché to the British diplomatic mission in 1946–50. Professor of Far Eastern History at the Australian National University, Fitzgerald puts forth a thesis of Chinese history and culture that is as straightforward as it is thought-provoking; continuity, as distinguished from immobility, is a dominant characteristic of the Chinese. In his book on modern Chinese history, excerpted below, he dwells on the theme that the Chinese revolution in the twentieth century is the product of its own society, which has recently completed another cycle of three stages: (1) the crumbling of the old order, (2) the search for a new pattern of society, and (3) the reappearance of the fundamental, though adapted, concepts of Chinese society. Questioning democracy as the "proper aim" of Chinese revolution at the present time, he considers the Kuomintang's failure as having been caused, among factors of lack of vision and long-term policy, by its inability to move either forward to modernity or back to Chinese tradition. The Kuomintang was buried, as it were, under the weight of the inevitable process of the Chinese historical spiral.

CHINESE of the second half of the nineteenth century . . . saw that the whole fabric of their culture and life was threatened by the innovations which the West either forced upon them at the cannon's mouth, or spread with the allures of commerce and education. Some thought that China must shut her doors more closely and make a supreme effort to expel the germ of change. Others, recognizing the inevitable, hoped to adopt just so much innovation as was necessary to resist the onrush of the rest. A few, a growing number, came to think that Chinese culture stood condemned; that all must be changed, that only by the outright adoption of every Western trait could the Chinese be saved. This view came to prevail. It was believed by the early revolutionaries that China must be entirely reshaped on the Western pattern, must become a nation State, and cease to pretend she was a universal empire; must also become a democracy, because that was modern, too, and must be industrialized so as to have the strength to contend with the rest of the inhabitants of the political jungle.

These were, and perhaps to many Chinese still are, the aims of the Revolution, the imperative needs which any change must satisfy. Yet it may be asked, and perhaps the answer will explain some of the contradictions of the Chinese Revolution, whether these aims were attainable, or in the Chinese world really desirable. Could the Chinese Revolution, inevitable

Charles P. Fitzgerald, *Revolution in China* (London: The Cresset Press, 1952), pp. 24–32, 71–74, 81, 117–18. Reprinted by permission.

though it was, have made China a great democracy, and was such an end the proper aim of the Revolution?

The idea of law, of human rights written in uncontestable covenants played a most signficant part in the origin of Western democratic thinking. So, too, in another way, did the Christian doctrine of the individual soul, the equal of any other soul. From these complex factors emerged the institutions which had in them the germs of democratic freedom. From the rediscovered literature of the classical past came a theory with which to adorn and justify these new liberties as a revival of the ancient democracy of Athens. And from the city-states, themselves a product of the Mediterranean environment, came that power of money as opposed to land which nourished the early growth of democracy, and later succumbed to the full-grown monster. The Western world came to accept this as a natural and indeed inevitable sequence of events; it was not perceived that it was in fact a series only possible in the peculiar setting of Europe, and wholly without application to other regions.

In China not one of the causes which gave birth to Western democracy operated. The universal Empire at a very early date, a date prior to the rise of the Roman Empire, extinguished for ever the rudimentary national States of the Far East and made each and all a province of the abiding Empire. War became civil war, and morally wrong. The rebel against the Empire was either a failure, in which case he was branded through history as a traitor, or successful, in which case he took over the Empire and became the legitimate ruler. In no case was he a patriot struggling for freedom. No sense of freedom as against tyranny animated the rebels of Chinese history. Their purpose was to capture the Empire, and then reform it, not to escape from it.

The fundamental requisites for democracy were thus lacking, and to supply them would have required a revolution even more profound than that which has taken place. If the fragmentation of Europe into nation-States after the fall of Rome is the first cause of European ideas of liberty, the main preoccupation of the Chinese reformers, as of the conservatives, was how to preserve the Empire. If the Empire had been broken up, or reduced to some federal constitution, it would have at once become the prey of the imperialist powers, who eagerly anticipated such a development. The introduction of a legal system surrounded by the hoary veneration which law has acquired in Europe was obviously impossible. Any legal system had to be brand new. As such it was without sanction of custom, without prestige and without effect.

The growth of individualism in a nation which had thought in terms of clan responsibility for two or three thousand years meant a shedding of responsibility to the clan without the assumption of any duty to the community. . . .

The overthrow of orthodoxy, of authoritarian doctrine, so essential if democracy is to be real, if the free play of ideas is to be allowed to form policy and advocate changes however sweeping, meant in China the simultaneous overthrow of moral standards. Confucianism was another monolith; ethics, morals, politics intricately bound together, inseparable, and clinging to the Empire like ivy to a tree. If Confucian doctrine was no longer sacred, then the bonds of filial obedience, of honesty and fair dealing were also deprived of sanctity; and if loyalty, the supreme Confucian virtue, were to be deprived of its object, the Throne, then no public virtue could survive.

The idea of patriotism, love of country, is not in China an ancient concept. Loyalty to the dynasty meant also, of course, loyalty to China, to civilization, and was so obvious a duty, so natural a sentiment of any thinking being, that it was not separated from its constituent ideas. The dynasty was China; China was the civilized world. No one would be loyal to barbarians rather than to China, and so the concept of patriotism lacked a contradiction and was left unexpressed.

Such were the causes which were leading the old Empire to destruction and revolution, and such were the obstacles in the way of a democratic State emerging from that revolution. It was thus inevitable that the revolution, which, once started by the changed circumstances of the Chinese world, could never be arrested half-way, must go through three main phases. First a period of increasing anarchy during which the pillars and bastions of the old order successively fell. Then a search, often enough down blind alleys, for a new pattern for society, a new theory of civilization. Finally, the search having shown that all other patterns were cut to suit very different communities, the reappearance of the fundamental concepts of Chinese society in a form fitted to the changed world.

These concepts are: a world sovereign authority, the old Empire, co-terminous with civilization; a balanced economy by which only luxuries and surplus products are exchanged, the basic industries and basic transportation being managed by the State; the establishment of an orthodox doctrine which harmonizes all the activities of the human being and provides a code of ethics, of politics, and of every other activity, including economics. This orthodox doctrine not only enshrines the aims and ideals of the Empire but also provides a means of selecting for its service the able and loyal members of the intellectual class.

In these old Chinese ideas, whether in their ancient form or in new guise, there is no place for freedom as the West understands it, no place for salvation as the Christian understands it, and no place for individualism as the Liberal would have it. But the old Chinese ideas fit very well to the new pattern. Loyalty to a doctrine, belief in the one world order which is civilization, and beyond which is either treason or barbarism, the duty to serve the sovereign authority, the importance of the clan — or the party — the subordinate role of the individual as such,

If it be true that the Chinese Revolution has ended in a new version of the ancient society, expanded beyond the limits of the Chinese Empire, embracing not Confucianism but Marxism, equally contemptuous of outer "barbarians," and equally self-satisfied with the new orthodoxy which time has not yet proved inadequate, this is, seen in perspective, a very natural conclusion.

The Empire was forced into revolution not because the Chinese themselves were discontented with their way of life, but because outside changes, sea-power and navigation, the conquest of the steppes, altered the basic conditions of their autarchic world and made it too small to survive. Very well, the old Chinese world was too small, but nothing had happened to convince the Chinese of the inadequacy of their concept. The scale was too small; then make it bigger; the Chinese Communists, embracing a world authoritarian doctrine in place of one local to China, have enlarged the arena in which old Chinese ideas can once more be put into practice, in more modern guise, expanded to the new scale, but fundamentally the same ideas which inspired the builders of the Han Empire and the restorers of the T'ang.[1]

The Communist insurrection could have been contained, perhaps subdued, if the Government, in the rural areas which it fully controlled — the vast majority of the provinces — had put into effect a real policy of land reform. The reduction of rents, remission and honest collection of taxes, measures to provide the peasant with loans at moderate interest, some resettlement and some redistribution of land, all measures which elsewhere have been the surest shield against Communism, all these were possible, quite practicable, but neglected.

But there was something else which ate out the heart of the Nationalist movement: the lack of any real satisfying and inspiring ideology. Nationalism was not enough, especially when it meant in practice yielding to the Japanese. Democracy was manifestly

---

[1] Han dynasty, 202 B.C.–A.D. 220; T'ang dynasty, 618–907. [Editor's note.]

not the ideal or the practice of the regime; it repudiated the past, yet seemed to hanker after Confucianism; it was not Christian, although many of its leaders were baptized Christians. To what end, to what vision of the future, the Kuomintang progressed, no one really knew. Not many of its members cared.

The short-term prospect, the rewards and spoils of office, the ambition of high command, all these things were eagerly sought and fiercely contested, but when it was asked where all was tending, when the provisional character of the Government would end, what ultimate shape it would assume, all was uncertain. Government propaganda and school indoctrination confined itself to a narrow and unintelligent nationalism more often concerned with criticism of the Western nations than of the Japanese. The Chinese are a highly intelligent people; it is not possible to enlist their co-operation in this way. The intellectuals withdrew from politics; the careerists controlled the party and strove to secure the favour of the Generalissimo, upon whom all depended.

The Chinese people are not averse to the personal rule of an autocrat; they had accepted the Empire for thousands of years. They now accept the "leadership," as it is euphemistically called, of Mao Tse-tung. But with this acceptance goes respect; it is necessary for the autocrat to show plainly that he knows his job, that he is the master of the Empire, not merely the manipulator of intrigues, the arbiter of factions. Chiang Kai-shek never really controlled China; he could not prevent Japanese infiltration, he could not crush the Communists, he could not discipline the Kuangsi generals nor keep Canton loyal; he juggled with the factions of the Kuomintang, but only ruled by playing one off against the other. A military ruler to command respect must be successful in war; a civilian autocrat must, like Stalin, construct an instrument of government both efficient and loyal. Chiang was an unsuccessful general; his party was neither loyal nor efficient.

Under the Kuomintang the worst evils of the warlord era were reduced, or eliminated. The internal situation did not seriously deteriorate, but it did not improve. The external situation changed for the worse. Instead of the limited encroachments of the Western powers, anxious for trade openings, for profitable concessions and special rights, but not at all anxious to take over the immense task of conquering and governing China — in place of these gadflies, the Kuomintang faced Japan, who did in fact intend to conquer China and to incorporate the whole Empire in her own.

The Kuomintang never faced this danger or made a policy to meet and counter it. They refused to see that to oppose Japan, which really did threaten, it was wise to conciliate the Western powers who did not. They failed to understand the change which the first world war had wrought in the West. The European powers were now faintly ashamed of their aggressions of the past. Their active Left parties were openly critical of "imperialism." These nations were now no longer any danger to China; it was not a question of whether they would seek new rights and concessions, but of how long it would be before they gave up what still remained to them.

Moreover, the West was now aware that democracy was on the defensive; it was prepared to encourage, even to aid in resistance to totalitarian aggression. America was no longer the aloof self-contained country of the early Republican period. America was already moving towards that contest for the Pacific which Japan also foresaw. The true policy for the Kuomintang was to place themselves unequivocally on the side of the democracies; to introduce those reforms which would convince the West that China had the same faith, and to show such resistance to the Japanese as to bring close the danger of a widespread war. The West was anxious to maintain peace; the prospect of a war throughout China, and one which might perhaps engulf the Eastern possessions of the West, would have stimulated the European and American leaders to take active steps to restrain Japan.

Instead, the obvious trend in China towards Fascism, the preference for German advisers in the military sphere, the weak yielding to Japan which gave no promise of national survival, and the continued covert hostility to the Westerner which the Kuomintang constantly displayed, these traits cooled the interest of the West, and induced the widespread belief that China was doomed to succumb to Japan, that there was no sense in engaging in a quarrel which China would not support, and that neutrality was the best policy for the Western nations. When the war came, China was left alone.

The Kuomintang was, of course, to a large extent the prisoner of its own past and of the still-decaying ancient Chinese social system. It strove to arrest the course of the revolution, to stabilize society while the necessary basis did not yet exist. The attempt to modernize China without interfering with the land system, the endeavour to fit some rags of Confucian doctrine to a party dictatorship, which itself was supposed to be temporary, to deny the practice of democracy and still pretend to be preparing the people for it, to proclaim and teach nationalism, and yield to the national enemy, this medley of contradictions could not form a coherent policy which would win mass support. The Kuomintang failed for lack of vision, for lack of any long-term policy thought out in terms of reality, and thus became a prey to selfish ambitions, to corruption and to nepotism.

. . . The failure to follow the revolution through, to carry it to the villages, and complete the task, was now shown to be the fatal error of the Nanking Government, and the ultimate cause of its downfall.

In 1945 the only hope for peace was in the agreement of the two main parties, but that agreement was impossible so long as one party worked for revolution and the other for reaction. The scholars were lost to the Kuomintang through its corruption, nepotism, misgovernment and inefficiency. They were won by the Communists, who in a long period of exile and hardship had learned to practise moderation, to govern honestly and to build a disciplined army. The Kuomintang had lost the road to democracy, and the Communists had travelled far from the pattern of the Russian Revolution. Thus the scholars and the peasants found they could give support to the Communists, and could not survive under the Kuomintang.

Neither party offered the Chinese people democratic government. The ideals of 1911 were forgotten. The Chinese people looked now for a Government which could govern, which knew its mind, had power and purpose, a theory and a practice which fitted together — in fact for a modern version of the government under which they had lived for so many centuries. The totalitarian aspect of the Communist regime does not dismay the Chinese people: the Empire was also totalitarian, though the word was not then coined. It was absolute, and so is Communism; it was hierarchic, ruling through a chosen group of specially trained men, the Confucian "Mandarin." So is Communism, ruling by its party, who are brought up on Marx and form a class apart. The Empire had its doctrine, its total explanation of philosophy, politics and economics; the teaching of Confucius. So has Communism, for which Marx as interpreted by Lenin, Stalin and Mao Tse-tung explains all and justifies everything.

So the Revolution went full circle, the old order fell, chaos followed its collapse, until from the fundamental forces of Chinese life and thought a new order, borrowing forms more than ideas from abroad, but claiming modernity by virtue of its foreign dress, has arisen to restore the Chinese Empire in the form of the People's Republic. As ever in China, form does not matter, but content is all important.

Dialectical Progression in Chinese History

MAO TSE-TUNG

Mao Tse-tung (1893–), an active Marxist at the time of the inception of the Chinese Communist Party in 1921, has been its undisputed leader and chief ideologue since the establishment of the party's new power base in Yenan in 1935–36. In this article, written jointly with "several other comrades" in December 1939, he outlines the course of Chinese history in unmistakably Marxist terms, making it perfectly clear that the ultimate goal of the Chinese revolution is socialism and communism under the leadership of the party of the proletariat. It is noteworthy that, while Mao takes cognizance of the international character of the Chinese Communist movement, he develops his thesis in the context not of world revolution, but of China's "glorious revolutionary tradition" and "splendid historical heritage." This essay, in keeping with the existing party line of the United Front, makes no direct criticisms of the Kuomintang. Yet it is equally significant that Chiang Kai-shek, the nationally recognized leader of the Anti-Japanese War, is nowhere mentioned. The only tribute to the Kuomintang is a reference to the so-called "Three People's Principles of the New Democracy" of Sun Yat-sen.

What precisely, then, is the historical role ascribed to the Kuomintang? How can Chiang's leadership in the Anti-Japanese War be construed? China at the time of the Anti-Japanese War, Mao says, is already in the first stage — the bourgeois-democratic or New Democratic stage as distinguished from the proletarian-socialist stage — of the twofold Chinese revolutionary movement, the leadership of both of which resides inevitably with the Chinese Communist Party. If *revolutionary* leadership inheres in the Communist Party during the New Democratic stage, is not the *political* leadership of the Kuomintang in the Anti-Japanese War something of an anachronism? What is to be said of the Kuomintang leadership at the conclusion of the war? This essay does not address itself explicitly to these questions, but a definite line of interpretation can be inferred from Mao's highly dialectical analysis of the basic character of the Chinese revolution and of the Kuomintang's class composition.

The New Democratic revolution, according to Mao, included, among other things, two principal contradictions, that "between feudalism and the great masses of the people" and that "between imperialism and the Chinese nation." Of the two, the contradiction more immediately operative during the Anti-Japanese War was that of the nation against imperialism. It was in this context that the anachronism of the Kuomintang *political* leadership during the war was justified.

In regard to class composition, the Kuomintang was recognized as a party principally of the bourgeoisie and the landlord, and the leadership within the party was said to be in the hands of the "big bourgeoisie" and the "big landlord." But while the Kuomintang leadership was by nature "semi-feudal" and "semi-colonial," its immediate class interests were by no means uniform. A segment of the Kuomintang leadership — the Wang Ching-weis — was more semi-colonial than semi-feudal, thus allying itself with the Japanese imperialists to become enemies of the people. However, another segment — unnamed, but Mao clearly points to the Chiang Kai-sheks — remained patriotic, being more semi-feudal than semi-colonial. It was on this basis that Chiang, who was said to represent the Anti-Japanese segment of the "big bourgeoisie" and "big landlord," was recognized, in the patriotic interest of the Chinese nation, as the national *political* leader during the course of the war.

92

The inference is clear that after the conclusion of the war, the basically reactionary Kuomintang must not be continued in its *political* leadership of the nation. When the "contradiction between feudalism and the great masses of the people" re-emerged after the war as the more immediate of the two principal contradictions, the Chiang Kai-sheks would have to be combated in the interest of the *revolutionary* leadership of the Chinese Communist Party, the vanguard of the proletariat. Hence, Mao was perfectly consistent, and acting in good faith, as it were, when he characterized Chiang on August 13th, only three days after the surrender of Japan became known, as "China's fascist ringleader, autocrat and traitor to the people." The dynamics of Communist logic was to leave the Kuomintang leadership behind.

D EVELOPING along the same lines as many other nations of the world, the Chinese nation (chiefly the Hans) first went through some tens of thousands of years of life in classless primitive communes. Up to now approximately 4,000 years have passed since the collapse of the primitive communes and the transition to class society, first slave society and then feudalism. . . . China . . . is therefore one of the oldest civilised countries in the world.

The Chinese nation is not only famous throughout the world for its stamina and industriousness, but also as a freedom-loving people with a rich revolutionary tradition. The history of the Hans, for instance, shows that the Chinese people would never submit to rule by the dark forces and that in every case they succeeded in overthrowing or changing such a rule by revolutionary means. In thousands of years of the history of the Hans, there have been hundreds of peasant insurrections, great or small, against the régime of darkness imposed by the landlords and nobility. And it was peasant uprisings that brought about most dynastic changes. All the nationalities of China have always rebelled against the foreign yoke and striven to shake it off by means of resistance. They accept a union on the basis of equality, not the oppression of one nationality by another. In thousands of years of history of the Chinese nation many national heroes

and revolutionary leaders have emerged. So the Chinese nation is also a nation with a glorious revolutionary tradition and a splendid historical heritage.

Although China is a great nation with a vast territory, an immense population, a long history, a rich revolutionary tradition and a splendid historical heritage, yet she remained sluggish in her economic, political and cultural development after her transition from the slave system into the feudal system. This feudal system, beginning from the Chou and Ch'in dynasties,[1] lasted about 3,000 years.

In feudal society, the main contradiction is between the peasantry and the landlord class.

And in this society the peasants and the handicraftsmen alone formed the principal classes that created wealth and culture.

. . . In the latter half of the nineteenth century, owing to the stimulus of foreign capitalism and certain breaches in the feudal economic structure, some merchants, landlords and bureaucrats started investing in modern industries. . . . At the turn of the century, China's national capitalism developed in a rudimentary form. Then, . . . during the first imperialist world war, China's own industry, chiefly textiles and flour milling, developed further because the European and American imperialist coun-

[1] Chou dynasty, c. 1027–256 B.C.; Ch'in dynasty, 221–206 B.C. [Editor's note.]

Mao Tse-tung, "The Chinese Revolution and the Chinese Communist Party," *Selected Works of Mao Tse-tung*, III (1954) pp. 73–84, 96–101. By permission of International Publishers Company, Inc.

tries, preoccupied with the war, temporarily relaxed their oppression of China.

The process of emergence and development of China's national capitalism has been at the same time the process of the emergence and development of China's bourgeoisie and proletariat. Just as certain sections of the merchants, landlords and bureaucrats were predecessors of the Chinese bourgeoisie, so certain sections of the peasants and handicraftsmen were predecessors of the Chinese proletariat. The Chinese bourgeoisie and proletariat, as two distinct social classes, are new-born classes which never existed before in Chinese history. In embryo in feudal society, they evolved into new social classes. They are interlinked but antagonistic classes, the twins born of China's old (feudal) society. However, the emergence and development of the Chinese proletariat accompanied not only the emergence and development of the Chinese national bourgeoisie, but also the imperialists' direct operation of enterprises in China. As a result, a very large section of the Chinese proletariat has a much longer standing and more experience than the Chinese bourgeoisie, and so it is a greater social force with a broader social foundation.

Yet this fresh change represented by the emergence and development of capitalism constitutes only one aspect of the change that has taken place since imperialist penetration into China. There is another aspect which co-exists with it as well as hampers it, namely, the collusion of foreign imperialism with China's feudal forces to arrest the development of Chinese capitalism.

. . . By penetrating into China the imperialist powers have on the one hand accelerated the disintegration of China's feudal society, caused factors of capitalism to emerge in China and transformed the feudal society into a semi-feudal one, and on the other hand imposed their ruthless rule on China and reduced an independent China into a semi-colonial and colonial China.

To sum up both aspects, this colonial, semi-colonial and semi-feudal society of ours possesses the following characteristics:

1. The foundation of the self-sufficing natural economy of feudal times is destroyed, but the exploitation of the peasantry by the landlord class — the basis of feudal exploitation — not only remains intact but is linked with the exploitation of comprador and usurer capital, and holds an obviously dominant position in China's social-economic life.

2. National capitalism has developed to a certain extent and played a considerable part in China's political and cultural life, but it has not become the principal social-economic form in China; quite feeble in strength, it is mostly tied in varying degrees to both foreign imperialism and domestic feudalism.

3. The autocratic rule of the emperors and the nobility has been overthrown, and in its place have arisen first the rule of the warlords and bureaucrats of landlord-class origin and then the joint dictatorship of the landlord class and the big bourgeoisie. In the occupied areas there is the rule of Japanese imperialism and its puppets.

4. Imperialism controls not only China's vital financial and economic arteries but also her political and military power. In the occupied areas everything is monopolised by Japanese imperialism.

5. China's economic, political and cultural development shows an extreme unevenness, because China has been under the rule, complete or partial, of several imperialist powers, because she has actually been in a prolonged state of disunity, and because her territory is immense.

6. Owing to the twofold oppression of imperialism and feudalism, and especially to the all-out offensive of Japanese imperialism, the broad masses of the Chinese people, particularly the peasants, have become more and more impoverished and have gone bankrupt in large numbers, living in hunger and cold and utterly deprived of political rights. Such extreme poverty and utter lack of freedom as the

Chinese people have known are rare throughout the world.

These are the characteristics of China's colonial, semi-colonial and semi-feudal society.

This situation has been brought about mainly by Japanese and other imperialist forces; it is the result of the combination of foreign imperialism and domestic feudalism.

The contradiction between imperialism and the Chinese nation, and the contradiction between feudalism and the great masses of the people, are the principal contradictions in modern Chinese society. Of course there are other contradictions, such as the contradictions between the bourgeoisie and the proletariat and the contradictions within the reactionary ruling classes themselves. The contradiction between imperialism and the Chinese nation, however, is the principal one among the various contradictions. The struggles arising from these contradictions and their intensification inevitably result in the daily-developing revolutionary movements. The great revolutions of modern and contemporary China have emerged and developed on the basis of these fundamental contradictions.

Since the character of present-day Chinese society is colonial, semi-colonial and semi-feudal, then what after all are our chief targets or enemies at this stage of the Chinese revolution?

They are none other than imperialism and feudalism, namely, the bourgeoisie of the imperialist countries and the landlord class at home. For these and none other are the principal agents that carry out oppression in Chinese society at the present stage and obstruct its advance. These agents conspire to oppress the Chinese people and, since national oppression by imperialism is the heaviest oppression, imperialism has become the foremost and fiercest enemy of the Chinese people.

Since Japan's armed invasion of China, the principal enemies of the Chinese revolution have been Japanese imperialism and all the collaborators and reactionaries who are in collusion with it, who have either openly capitulated or are prepared to capitulate.

The Chinese bourgeoisie, also actually oppressed by imperialism, once led revolutionary struggles; it played a principal leading role, for instance, in the Revolution of 1911, and also joined such revolutionary struggles as the Northern Expedition and the present Anti-Japanese War. In the long period from 1927 to 1937, however, the upper stratum of the bourgeoisie, as represented by the reactionary bloc of the Kuomintang, was in league with imperialism and formed a reactionary alliance with the landlord class, turning against the friends who had helped it — the Communist Party, the proletariat, the peasantry and other sections of the petty bourgeoisie, betraying the Chinese revolution and thereby causing its defeat. At that time, therefore, the revolutionary people and their political party, the Communist Party, could only regard these bourgeois elements as a target of the revolution. During the Anti-Japanese War a section of the big landlords and the big bourgeoisie, as represented by Wang Ching-wei, has already deserted to the enemy and turned collaborator. Consequently the anti-Japanese people can only regard these big bourgeois, who have betrayed our national interests, as a target in the revolution.

What, after all, is the character of the Chinese revolution at the present stage? Is it a bourgeois-democratic or a proletarian-socialist revolution? Obviously, not the latter but the former.

It is now clear that Chinese society is still a colonial, semi-colonial and semi-feudal society, that the principal enemies of the Chinese revolution are still imperialism and the feudal forces, that the task of the Chinese revolution consists in a national revolution and a democratic revolution for overthrowing these two principal enemies, and furthermore that the bourgeoisie sometimes also takes part in this revolution and that, even if the big bourgeoisie betrays the revolution and becomes its enemy, the spearhead of the revolution will still be directed at imperialism and feudalism rather than at capitalism and capitalist private property in general. That being so, the character of the Chinese revolution at the present stage is not proletarian-socialist but bourgeois-democratic.

However, the bourgeois-democratic revolution in present-day China is no longer of the general, old type, which is now obsolete, but one of a special, new type. This kind of revolution is developing in China as well as in all colonial and semi-colonial countries, and we call it the new-democratic revolution. This new-democratic revolution is part of the world proletarian-socialist revolution, which resolutely opposes imperialism, i.e., international capitalism. Politically it means the joint dictatorship of several revolutionary classes over the imperialists, collaborators and reactionaries, and opposition to the transformation of Chinese society into a society under bourgeois dictatorship. Economically, it means nationalisation of all big capital and big enterprises of the imperialists, collaborators and reactionaries, distribution of the land of the landlords among the peasants, and at the same time the general preservation of private capitalist enterprises without the elimination of rich-peasant economy. While clearing the way for capitalism, this democratic revolution of a new type creates the pre-condition for socialism. The present stage of the Chinese revolution is a transitional stage between putting an end to the colonial, semi-colonial and semi-feudal society and establishing a socialist society — a process of new-democratic revolution. This process, begun only after the First World War and the Russian October Revolution, started in China with the May 4 Movement of 1919. A new-democratic revolution is a revolution of the broad masses of the people led by the proletariat and directed against imperialism and feudalism. China must go through this revolution before she can advance to a socialist society; otherwise she cannot advance to socialism.

This kind of new-democratic revolution differs greatly from the democratic revolutions in the history of European and American countries, in that it results not in the dictatorship of the bourgeoisie, but in the dictatorship of the united front of all revolutionary classes under the leadership of the proletariat. During the Anti-Japanese War, the anti-Japanese democratic political power built up in the anti-Japanese base areas under the leadership of the Chinese Communist Party is a political power of the Anti-Japanese National United Front, which is neither a one-class dictatorship of the bourgeoisie nor a one-class dictatorship of the proletariat, but a joint dictatorship of several revolutionary classes under the leadership of the proletariat. All those who stand for resistance to Japan and for democracy are qualified to share this political power, regardless of their party affiliations.

This kind of new-democratic revolution differs also from a socialist revolution in that it aims only at overthrowing the rule of the imperialists, collaborators and reactionaries in China, but not at injuring any capitalist sections which can still take part in the anti-imperialist, anti-feudal struggles.

This kind of new-democratic revolution is basically in line with the revolution of the Three People's Principles as advocated by Sun Yat-sen in 1924. In the Manifesto of the First National Congress of the Kuomintang issued in that year, Sun Yat-sen stated:

The so-called democratic system in modern nations is usually monopolised by the bourgeoisie and has simply become an instrument for oppressing the common people. As to the Principle of Democracy of the Kuomintang, it stands for something to be shared by all the common people and not to be monopolised by a few.

Further:

Enterprises, whether Chinese-owned or foreign-owned, which are monopolistic in character or which are on too large a scale for private management, such as banks, railways and air lines, shall be operated by the state, so that private capital cannot dominate the livelihood of the people: This is the main principle of the control of capital.

And again in his Testament, Sun Yat-sen pointed out the fundamental principle for domestic and foreign policies:

. . . We must arouse the masses of the people and unite in a common fight with those nations of the world who treat us on the basis of equality. . . .

The Three People's Principles of the old democracy adapted to old circumstances at home and abroad were thus remoulded into the Three People's Principles of the New Democracy adapted to new circumstances at home and abroad. . . .

Since China's bourgeois-democratic revolution at the present stage is not a bourgeois-democratic revolution of the general, old type, but a democratic revolution of a special, new type, a new-democratic revolution, and since furthermore the Chinese revolution is now taking place in the new international setting of the 1930's and 1940's, characterised by the rise of socialism and the decline of capitalism, and in the period of the Second World War and of revolutions, there can be no doubt whatever that the ultimate perspective of the Chinese revolution is not capitalism but socialism and communism.

To complete China's bourgeois-democratic revolution (the new-democratic revolution) and to prepare to transform it into a socialist revolution when all the necessary conditions are present — that is the sum total of the great and glorious revolutionary task of the Communist Party of China. All members of the Party should strive for its accomplishment and should never give up half-way. Some immature Communists think that we have only the task of the democratic revolution at the present stage, but not that of the socialist revolution at the future stage; or that the present revolution or the agrarian revolution is in fact the socialist revolution. It must be emphatically pointed out that both views are erroneous. Every Communist must know that the whole Chinese revolutionary movement led by the Chinese Communist Party is a complete revolutionary movement embracing the two revolutionary stages, democratic and socialist, which are two revolutionary processes differing in character, and that the socialist stage can be reached only after the democratic stage is completed. The democratic revolution is the necessary preparation for the socialist revolution, and the socialist revolution is the inevitable trend of the democratic revolution. And the ultimate aim of all Communists is to strive for the final building of socialist society and communist society. We can give correct leadership to the Chinese revolution only on the basis of a clear understanding of both the differences between the democratic and socialist revolutions and their interconnections.

The Chinese Revolution
in a World Communist Setting

G. ASTAFYEV

Voprosy Istorii, journal of the Historical Institute of the Academy of Sciences of the USSR, gives the Soviet interpretation of the Chinese revolution in an article by G. Astafyev. The course of the New Democratic revolution in China, the author explains, is "predetermined" by three cardinal historical factors: one, the combination of semi-colonial and semi-feudal oppression; two, the emergence of the leadership of the Chinese Communist Party in the Chinese national liberation movement; and three, the revolutionary experience and total support of the Soviet Union.

Writing in 1949, Astafyev made explicit a number of Marxist historical truths (which would hardly have been prudent for Mao to stress ten years earlier under a vastly different set of concrete circumstances): that the Kuomintang had forfeited its *revolutionary* leadership in the national liberation movement in April 1927, when its bourgeois-landlord bloc launched a civil war against the worker-peasant bloc; that the Kuomintang became increasingly reactionary during the Anti-Japanese War in proportion as its landlord elements, best exemplified by the "four families" of Chiang, Ch'en, Soong and Kung, gained an ascendancy over the bourgeois elements; and that American imperialism, in league with the "four families," had a continuing interest in the political and economic exploitation of China. This essay is also noteworthy for its obvious effort to minimize the role of Mao and the Chinese Communist Party at the same time as it seeks to magnify Stalin's "profound theoretical analysis" of the Chinese revolution and Russia's unique contributions to world progress. It was not until after August 1945, when the "Soviet and Mongol" troops entered into the Far Eastern phase of the Second World War, the essay makes clear, that the Chinese Communists, "taking advantage" of the victorious offensive of their international comrades, were able to successfully consolidate their position. The Chinese revolution, no different from the revolutions in Central and Eastern Europe, can be properly understood only in the light of the "ingenious" expositions of Lenin and Stalin and must be viewed as an aspect of the inexorable logic of world history at the present stage.

I N the year 1927 Comrade Stalin pointed out the "semi-colonial status of China and the financial-economic domination of imperialism" as being one of the basic factors determining the situation in China. His words continued to retain full signifi-cance in 1937, when Japan burst into North and Central China.

The heroic struggle which progressive elements of the Chinese people, headed by the proletariat and directed by the Communist Party, have been waging for these past

G. Astafyev, "Uspexi kitaikogo naroda v bor'be za nezavisimost' i demokratiiu," *Voprosy Istorii*, No. 5 (May 1949), pp. 26–31, 35–37, 44, 51, selections. This translation is adapted from the English rendition that appears in the *Soviet Press Translations*, IV, No. 22 (December 15, 1949), pp. 675–95, under the title of "The Achievements of the Chinese People in Their Struggle for Independence and Democracy." The editor is ably assisted by Mr. James Rice of the University of Chicago in the preparation of this selection.

ten years against the combined forces of imperialism and internal reaction, still could not bring about the collapse of imperialist domination in China.

Imperialism held sway in China with the support of the so-called compradore bourgeoisie — the intermediary between foreign capital and the Chinese market — and with the support of the semi-feudal classes and elements among the landlords, the usurious merchant bourgeoisie, and the military and civilian bureaucracy, which hold a monopoly of economic and political power in China, and which exploit the workers by the use of feudal and medieval methods.

Characterizing this power of the landlords and the bureaucracy, which is peculiarly associated with the existence of commercial capital and which borrows from them as feudal vestiges medieval methods of exploiting and oppressing the peasants, Comrade Stalin pointed out that they are the preponderant factors in the oppression of China.

This combination of semi-colonial and semi-feudal oppression, a nexus of the interests of both imperialism and the landlord-bourgeois top military clique, based on joint exploitation of the workers, was until recently one of China's characteristic features. This explains why the national liberation movement of the Chinese people was directed simultaneously against both modes of oppression — feudal and imperialist. Comrade Stalin notes this as the cardinal feature of the Chinese Revolution.

It was primarily the Chinese industrial proletariat and peasantry that experienced the double yoke of imperialism and feudal vestiges to the fullest extent. The petty urban bourgeoisie and a portion of the big bourgeoisie (its industrial element) likewise felt it to a certain degree. But as Comrade Stalin points out, the "big national bourgeoisie is extremely weak in China," dependent on imperialism, and frightened by the scope of the revolutionary movement. Consequently, the leadership of the Chinese national liberation movement

fell to the Chinese proletariat and its party, which is the second characteristic feature of the Chinese Revolution.

The Great October Socialist Revolution and the Soviet Union — the state of workers and peasants created by it — exercised a tremendous and decisive influence upon the development of the national liberation movement in China, as well as throughout the world.

The October Revolution burst the imperialist chains which fettered China, inspired the Chinese workers to struggle against imperialism, and provided them not only with all-out moral support and aid from the USSR, but also with the vast revolutionary experience of the Russian proletariat and its party. Comrade Stalin mentions this fact as the third characteristic feature of the Chinese Revolution.

All the above factors predetermined the basic disposition of class forces in China in the initial stage of the national liberation movement, when the "bloc of workers, peasants, bourgeois intelligentsia, and national bourgeoisie," who were politically united in the Kuomintang and in the Canton government, launched its campaign against foreign imperialism and the military-feudal dictatorship of the militarists.

In April 1927 the Chinese bourgeoisie betrayed the cause of national liberation and made a deal with the imperialists and the landlords. The petty bourgeois intelligentsia, which had also deserted to the camp of reaction, soon followed suit. From a party representing the anti-imperialist and anti-feudal bloc of revolutionary classes, the Kuomintang became the party of the reactionary, bourgeois-landlords' bloc, which established its dictatorship in the country with the aid of the imperialists and launched a civil war against the workers and peasants.

The struggle for national liberation entered its second stage, a "higher phase of its development, the phase of agrarian revolution." The characteristic feature of the second stage "is the fact that the revolution wreaks its fury primarily on internal enemies, most of all on the feudal lords and the feudal system," simultaneously maintaining its anti-imperialist bias. . . .

The intensification of Japanese aggression in China — the seizure of Manchuria in 1931, the attack on Shanghai in 1932, and the increased penetration into Inner Mongolia and North China in subsequent years — threatened the national independence and the very national existence of the Chinese people.

The tremendous danger threatening China could have been warded off only by mobilizing the forces of the entire nation, by unifying the people into a single nation-wide resistance front against imperialist plans for enslaving the country. The Chinese Communist Party, which headed the people's movement against Japanese aggression, was the leader and organizer of the united, national, anti-Japanese front. The Communist Party made repeated overtures to the Kuomintang to end the civil war and to create a united anti-Japanese front.

The Kuomintang, however, ignored these proposals; and only the treacherous Japanese attack on China of July 7, 1937, and the tremendous outburst of popular indignation it aroused, which testified to the people's determination to resist the Japanese invasion, compelled the Kuomintang to renounce its policy of sabotage and to agree, with great reluctance and considerable delay, to recognize the united front. . . .

During the course of the anti-Japanese war, the leading role of the Chinese proletariat and its Communist Party, and their influence among the broad masses of the Chinese people, continued to grow. The power and the importance of the united, national, anti-Japanese front, and the victories it won in armed resistance against the Japanese invaders and in democratic construction in the territories liberated from Japanese occupation, increased proportionately. The major changes in the economic and political situation of China caused by the war contributed to this. The Japanese seizure of the economically developed

coastal provinces and the restriction of Chinese Kuomintang territory to the backward and agrarian western provinces, brought about a change in the correlation of forces within the ruling camp — namely, the collapse of the role and the influence of the industrial bourgeoisie, and the strengthening of the role and influence of the landlord class and of the usurious merchant bourgeoisie closely associated with it. The landlords became the decisive force in the landlord-bourgeois bloc.

In conjunction with the waning influence of the national bourgeoisie and the waxing influence of the landlords, an ever more important role in the economy of Kuomintang China began to be played by the monopoly of the "four families," headed by Chiang Kai-shek, Ch'en Li-fu, T. V. Soong, and K'ung hsiang-hsi, who led the Kuomintang and the government of China which it controlled. Supported by the imperialists, these "four dynasties" of China amassed immense capital during the period of their domination, and took possession of a number of all-important posts in separate branches of China's economy. Particularly great opportunities for aggrandizement were afforded these "four families" during the war years. Under cover of military exigency, they not only established rigid control over the economic life of the country through appropriate government organizations, but also employed this control to subjugate the entire economy of the country to their own influence.

The political and economic domination of the "four families" is closely linked with the semi-feudal and semi-colonial status of China. The monopoly of the "four families" relies upon the landlord class, without which it could not exercise its dictatorship and exploit the workers of China. No less closely is it linked with foreign capital. The very process of its formation and growth proved possible only as a result of the direct political and economic support of the imperialist states, particularly the USA, which are interested in the enslavement and exploitation of China.

The entry of the USSR into the war with Japan in August 1945, the rapid destruction of the Japanese war machine, and the capitulation of Japan as a result of this entry, shattered the plans of international and Chinese reaction to crush the democratic movement of the Chinese people.

Taking advantage of the victorious offensive of Soviet and Mongol troops against the Japanese Kwantung Army, the Eighth People's Army of Liberation in North China and the Fourth People's Army of Liberation in Central China, with the aid of partisans and detachments of peasant defense units, opened a counter-offensive on August 10, 1945, against the Japanese forces and in a short period of time liberated a large number of cities and 350,000 square kilometers of territory with a population of 20,000,000 people.

As a result of the victory of the heroic Soviet people over German fascism and the entry of the USSR into the war with Japan, the speedy defeat of Japanese imperialism strengthened the military and political position of the democratic camp to a tremendous degree, and placed the problem of the democratization of all China on the agenda.

Immediately following the capitulation of Japan the Chinese Communist Party, having advanced a broad program of democratic reform for the postwar period, resumed its negotiations with the Kuomintang.

The self-sacrificing work of the Chinese Communist Party, based on the consistent policy of Marxism-Leninism, has not only enabled the Chinese people to hold their own in the war against Japan and to crush the schemes of reaction and American imperialism following the war, but has also led the majority of the Chinese people to recognize the democratic program of the Communist Party as the only correct path, leading to the liberation of the country from the shackles of imperialism and the fetters of feudalism, to the building of a free, independent, and democratic China that is strong, united, and flourishing. The Chinese Communist Party has extensively utilized the revolutionary experience accumulated by the Russian Bolsheviks; and its work is guided by the strategy and tactics of the revolutionary struggle as elaborated by Lenin and Stalin, the great leaders of the world proletariat. "The Communist Party of the Soviet Union is our best teacher, from whom we must learn," says Mao Tse-tung.

The works of Comrade Stalin, especially those dealing with the Chinese problem, have had the greatest significance in the formulation of the correct Marxist-Leninist policy of the Communist Party. In these works Comrade Stalin, on the basis of a profound theoretical analysis of the situation in China, defined the characteristic features of the Chinese Revolution, ingeniously predicted its course, and outlined the conditions for its success.

Today the Chinese Communist Party is already assigning the Chinese people a still broader task, to give the development of the entire national economy a planned character and, by raising the productivity of labor, gradually to improve the standard of living of the workers and the people, and thereby to consolidate the alliance of workers and peasants, to guarantee the leading role of the city in the administration of the village, and to lay the economic foundations for the transition to socialism. . . .

Just as in the countries of Central and Eastern Europe, the new democratic system developing in China is laying the groundwork "for the transition to a socialist path of development." . . .

The victory of the Chinese people's democracy means that the imperialist chain has been broken at its weak colonial link. By showing the backward colonial and dependent peoples the way to socialism, the victory of the people's democracy in China accelerates by leaps and bounds the triumph of democracy and socialism throughout the world, and hastens the collapse of the imperialist camp, the camp of the oppression and enslavement of peoples.

Kuomintang Overwhelmed by Forces of Social Change

JOHN K. FAIRBANK

John K. Fairbank (1907–   ), Francis Lee Higginson Professor of History and Director of East Asian Research Center at Harvard, spent seven years in China, concluding a variety of U. S. government services as Director of the United States Information Service in that country. His contribution to the dialogue on the Chinese revolution and the Kuomintang debacle lies in his synthetic approach to the problem, giving due attention to human factors and historical forces. The Kuomintang, he says, was a nationalistic reform party at the turn of the century, dedicated to the unification of the nation and the modernization of its government. Three problems presented themselves, however. First of all, as the Kuomintang derived much of its strength from the "literate upper stratum" and the "more modern elements of the old ruling class," it is but natural that, while the party espoused reforms of sort, it looked askance upon mass movements and "violent social change." Operating "within the framework of a conservative nationalism," the party sought to bring about only such political and economic measures as would not upset the traditional social order. It was, in other words, for reform from above, not revolution from below. Thus, the Kuomintang's ascendancy was attended by the revival of Confucianism "that lacked the intellectual vigor to gain the allegiance of thinking Chinese," the political control of education and the stifling of mass education, and incomplete and ineffectual programs of democratization and rural reconstruction. This whole set of issues, traceable to the nature and composition of the party, was compounded by a second problem, that of Japanese invasion. The war years witnessed the growing influence of the conservative landlords and militarists in the Kuomintang, a vicious inflationary spiral, increasing reliance on naked force rather than moral suasion, and shameful graft and self-seeking. The Kuomintang dictatorship, "while not an absolute power, became absolutely corrupted." In addition, there was the third problem of the challenge of the Chinese Communist Party, which neglected no opportunity to undermine the prestige of the Kuomintang and to expose it to public ridicule and contempt. The Communists established rapport with the intellectuals and won their respect by stressing civil liberties and social justices as political rights to be gained; they mobilized popular support by going to the people and espousing mass movements. Besides, the Communist Party had the advantage of not having to bear the brunt of the Sino-Japanese War, during which time it conserved its strength and advanced its own interests.

In sum, Professor Fairbank believes that the cause of the fall of the Kuomintang, made almost inevitable by these three sets of problems, is to be found in the party's "deep bureaucratic distrust of mass movements and popular initiative and an easily rationalized determination to retain power at any price." But he cautions the reader to eschew facile and "simple-minded" theorization — Chinese theory of dynastic cycle or Western theory of linear progress — for, as he says, "historical trends are no one's monopoly." What Fairbank does suggest is: human history, being human, does not have to be inevitable; at the same time, it is well to realize that historical forces do tend to condition, sometime decisively, the course of human drama, especially if the stage is set, as in the case of the Kuomintang rule in China, under the direction of an "uninstructable" leadership of "right-wing authoritarianism" unable either to mobilize or utilize forces of social change. In this connection, he points out that the history of modern China, with deep roots in its "im-memorial culture," could not have been controlled from without, by the Soviet Union or the U.S. Alien forces in China, to be effective, must be adopted by the Chinese themselves and attuned to the dynamics of Chinese history.

IN a general way it can be said that the Nationalist revolution of the 1920's combined the traditional trend toward re-unification of the country under a strong leader (in this case Chiang Kai-shek) with a new trend toward modernization of the government through the use of Western administrative methods, the inculcation of a new loyalty to the nation, and the mo-nopoly of power by a party dictatorship (rather than a new dynasty). The dom-inant sentiment behind the revolution was a nationalism which sought both unity within China and independence from for-eign domination. Its class basis was still, however, the literate upper stratum. Essen-tially, the Nanking Government in the decade after 1927 led the way in the mod-ernization of China's upper class institu-tions. But it was unable overnight to revo-lutionize the life of the common peasant.

When the Kuomintang inherited the mantle of central government, it was un-like its imperial predecessor in that it pos-sessed modern facilities for bringing its control down to the village level. The telephone and telegraph, motor roads and bus routes, linking local areas with the capital, gave Nanking and later Chungking the means of conveying their orders at once to the smallest hamlet, just as the growth of the modern money economy made them interested in revenue collected directly in all parts of the country. The new Nationalist Government became a center for the spread of reform to the vil-lages through agricultural extension, crop improvement, and other programs. Simul-taneously it tried to choke off peasant-based rebellion by an intensified police control. But once it ceased to foment violent social

change, it was foredoomed to govern from the top down. Trained modern personnel were lacking to build local self-government up to the provincial level; moreover such an effort might open the door to popular agitation and dissident movements; so Nan-king sought to build its central administra-tion down through the provinces to the village level.

. . . In 1939 the Nationalist Govern-ment issued a new statute to reorganize the *hsien*[1] and areas below it, in an attempt to check the increasing tendency toward bu-reaucratic government from the top down-ward. Beginning with the family house-hold it was provided that families should be grouped more flexibly, on community lines, to form *chia* and *pao*. A number of *pao* should then form villages or towns, which would in turn be under the *hsien* government. The villages and towns were now to become incorporated legal persons able to operate their own local administra-tions. Each *pao* should form an assembly and elect two representatives, who would in turn function in a village or town assem-bly. The latter would assist the head of the village or town government, who would himself be elected.

The result of this effort to inculcate some kind of democracy or at least popular participation through reform of adminis-tration was disappointing. Wartime circum-stances were highly unpropitious. More fundamental was the fact that this political reform was confined to the political sphere, unattended by change in the local social and economic structure in which it was expected to operate. On paper the law of

[1] County. [Editor's note.]

Reprinted by permission of the publishers from John King Fairbank, *The United States and China*, pp. 171, 188–94, 200–04, 209, 221–25, 245, 262–63, 310–13, Cambridge, Massachusetts: Har-vard University Press, Copyright, 1948, 1958 by the President and Fellows of Harvard College.

1939 was put into effect in nearly all the districts in Free China. Yet in the same period the military and police authorities dominated the scene. There is little record of the election process taking hold as a factor for active change. . . .

The growth of political controls through local gendarmerie, secret police, press censorship, subsidizing of education, the *pao-chia* and other devices, all supervised by the local Party office, was accompanied in Kuomintang China by a revival of traditional Confucianism. This doctrinal metamorphosis began by stressing the principle of nationalism and from it going back to the national heritage to find political doctrines which would support central power. . . .

By 1934 the state cult of Confucius was nominally revived. In the same year Chiang launched his New Life Movement to instill in his people a new social consciousness and martial spirit through a revival of the ancient virtues of moral conduct. These were *li*, variously defined as propriety, the principles of social usage, "proper behavior according to status," a regulated attitude; *i* (or *yi*), right conduct, justice; *lien*, integrity, and *ch'ih*, conscience, the sense of shame. Since these classical concepts were now vague at best, 96 specific rules were issued to apply them to the categories of food, clothing, shelter, and action: for example, do not eat noisily, correct your posture, stop smoking, keep your gown buttoned, do not spit, kill rats and flies, be prompt, use native products. Through a nation-wide network of some 1300 local associations, the movement sought paternalistically to lead each individual to practice orderliness and cleanliness. Many other activities proliferated under it in 1934–1937. Some of them were easy to ridicule but they represented nevertheless a direct attack on China's problem of social regeneration — in just the way that the commandant of a military academy might be expected to attempt it.

The revival of Confucianism was most actively promoted by Ch'en Li-fu, whose uncle had been Chiang Kai-shek's patron and who became Chiang's most loyal political organizer. . . .

In general Ch'en Li-fu called for the fusion of Western technology and Confucian social values. This echoed the nineteenth-century slogan, "Chinese studies as the fundamental structure, Western studies for practical use." Ch'en argued that ancient Chinese culture is the cure for modern China's ills. "The spirit of Confucianism is the means of adusting our culture to the modern age." He urged that the dicta of famous Confucian scholars be systematically arranged and explained to the people. "Confucianism belongs to no specific class." It is actually in keeping with Sun's Three Principles.

In active politics Ch'en Li-fu concentrated on the struggle against Communism. To compete with it on the plane of ideology he propounded a theory of "vitalism," set forth in a work of cosmology first presented as lectures at the Central Political Institute in 1933.

These ideas of Chiang and his henchman made no contribution to Chinese thought but had importance because they were held by the wielders of Kuomintang power. Modern-minded Chinese scholars could not find in their confused atavism any solution to the fundamental problems of China's adaptation to modern life. The right-wing authoritarianism of Chiang and Ch'en, though widely spread through school and Party, lacked the intellectual vigor to gain the allegiance of thinking Chinese.

. . . Ch'en Li-fu had become Minister of Education in 1938. During the next seven years of wartime austerity he came increasingly under liberal attack because of his evident use of the educational system for partisan political ends.

It had been apparent from the beginning that the Kuomintang considered education to be a tool of the state. The political thinking of the students of Free China was intimidated increasingly through the mechanism of the Kuomintang Youth Corps founded in 1938. Its branches were established within every student body with official support. As the Chungking government felt itself more and more on the defensive against the Communists, these branches made it their business to exalt the official ideology and control thought.

Mass education was meanwhile discountenanced. As a single example, take the experience of Dr. T'ao Hsing-chih (Heng-chi Tao), one of the great figures of modern Chinese education. After studying at the University of Illinois and with John Dewey at Columbia, T'ao had gone into rural education in China and helped develop the system whereby school children became teachers to other illiterates. . . . This literacy movement turned into a chain reaction, particularly during the united front of 1937–38 when the government was at Hankow. Evidently it seemed like political dynamite. Ch'en Li-fu called T'ao in and offered him the presidency of an agricultural college, suggesting that he should change his line of work. The little teacher movement was suppressed. T'ao opened a school for orphan children. At the time of his death in 1946 he was being threatened by the secret police for objecting to civil war. His genius as an educator inspired a whole generation, quite independently of the Communists, who now exploit his name.

After the war when the Nationalist Government moved back to the coastal cities, its problem of thought control was sharply intensified. The first jubilation over victory gave way to disillusionment, for liberation from Japan brought only further inflation and civil war. Middle schools and universities became centers of "dangerous thought," anti-corruption and anti-civil war. Arrests and disappearances of students and professors became frequent. Chinese education was turned into a battleground where indoctrination, secret police surveillance, starvation, terror, and the stirrings of revolution all but wiped out the nascent liberal tradition.

Given the record of corruption and terrorism which overtook the Kuomintang government in proportion as its problems multiplied and its leadership moved to the right, it is not surprising that the Chinese intelligentsia in their political thinking became steadily more estranged from it. The Chinese Communist Party was able more and more easily to recruit personnel from the student class, at the same time gaining the widespread tacit sympathy of intellectuals in education, the professions, and the lower levels of the bureaucracy. The Communist appeal to the intelligentsia was typically expressed in terms of the civil liberties and social justice so openly flouted by the Kuomintang police and bureaucrats. The resulting "desertion of the intellectuals" became a plainly marked phenomenon of the 1940's. In a country where the literati still stand so close to the government, this classic harbinger of revolution was more than usually significant.

In the early 1930's the lack of large-scale and effective Central Government aid for the villages was highlighted by a growing interest in the reconstruction of village economy. Several programs were set going in selected areas where the problems of peasant life were studied and methods developed for the promotion of literacy and improvement of living standards. In many of these efforts Christian missionaries had led the way. Best known to Westerners was the experiment financed partly by the Rockefeller Foundation at Ting-hsien in North China under the leadership of the dynamic Dr. Y. C. James Yen. Another model county was developed by the government near Nanking, and a pioneer effort of this type was also made by the scholar Liang Sou-ming in Shantung. Fundamentally, these were all reform efforts which tried to give the peasantry some education for citizenship, some public health service, and scientific improvements as in crop and animal breeding — precursors of India's community development programs of today.

The movement for rural reconstruction discovered very soon that the problems of economic livelihood were deeply imbedded in social and political institutions. It became plain that a higher standard of living was a prerequisite for any democratic processes of a Western type. Improvements in living standards in turn depended upon social change. For example, the scientific reforms attempted at Ting-hsien needed financial support greater than the peasantry could provide, peasant organizations in support of local improvements required official permission, the improvement of crops raised questions of rent and land tenure, an increase of literacy was likely to make the populace more vocal in the pressing of grievances.

In short, any real change in one aspect of the old order on the land implied fundamental changes in the whole system. The problems of the Chinese countryside were so far-reaching and the pressure for change so great that reforms were always likely to set off a chain reaction toward revolt. This interdependence of democracy and the people's livelihood was probably what led the Nationalist movement to stop short in its democratization program, after the achievement of power, lest it should provoke a political and economic revolution among the Chinese masses.

In retrospect it seems plain that the government at Nanking, as the first fruit of the Chinese Nationalist movement, had been caught between two forces. The one was aggressive Japanese militarism which sought to shatter its new unity and check all that it might accomplish in the upbuilding of a powerful Chinese state. The other force was that of a mass discontent which sought to remake the life of the Chinese people on the land.

Unhappily the very factors which gave Nanking its strength as a focus of nationalism seem to have prevented it from taking the leadership of the nascent mass revolution. For the spirit of patriotism had arisen first among the merchants and students of the upper class who constituted the modern face of the traditional landlord gentry. Compradors, merchants, and bankers in the treaty ports used capital derived from the rents of the hinterland and the perquisites of old-style officials. Modern students who led the way in patriotism came necessarily from upper-class backgrounds, rather than from the peasantry. China could not be remade in a day, and Sun Yat-sen's followers, after the overthrow of the imperial system and the warlords, had their hands full in creating the political superstructure of a new nation, with the support of the more modern elements of the old ruling class. In the long course of the revolution, Nanking represented the partial modernization of China's central government more than a broadening of its base.

When the Nationalist Government after 1937 moved from the seacoast to the interior of Szechwan, there was a corresponding shift in the nature of its support. The Szechwan landlords and militarists took the place of the Shanghai bankers. Although the financial and mercantile class of the treaty ports had maintained close ties with landlordism, it had been in the forefront of modernization and of the Nationalist movement and had supported reform, though not revolution, in the countryside. The landed magnates of the interior, on the other hand, were conservatives of an earlier generation. They interpreted the wartime slogan of "Resistance and Reconstruction" to mean resistance to social change and consolidation of their position, while the Communists interpreted it to mean the acquisition of power through resistance, revolution, and mass mobilization. As a result when the Nationalist leaders settled down at Chungking in 1938 they had to face the question whether to follow the current trend of the united front and base their power upon mass mobilization, or to leave the old order intact upon the land.

Wartime politics in China had some overtones of the passing of the Mandate of Heaven, modern style. The Nationalist Government's currency depreciated in a vicious spiral in which production was depressed in favor of speculation and hoarding, while unproductive expenditure was increased to finance the war. But this monetary inflation went hand in hand with a no less tragic depreciation of the government's prestige.

It is still true in China that a regime is sanctioned by its moral worth. A morally unworthy regime must rely upon force, instead of popular acquiescence in its rule. Like the old imperial administration, the Kuomintang government, in spite of the expanded number of its officials and the greater mobility and fire power of its armed forces, was still a rather small organization for so large a country. Its grip therefore depended partly on its prestige; and one constant aim of its Chinese Communist opponents was to undermine its moral repute, through radio and press as well as by more ancient methods of rumor and propaganda. In this the Communists had the greatest help from the bad record of the government itself. In meeting China's limitless problems it committed, through the person of its corrupt administrators, infinite mistakes. The postwar take-over process, when carpet-bagging generals and politicians returned to the coastal provinces and Formosa, was as shameful a record of official looting as modern history has displayed. The inflation made official salaries shrink out of sight. Graft took their place. But self-seeking and corruption seem to have been intensified by the officials' loss of confidence in the government's future. The result was a cynical *sauve-qui-peut*.

The government was thus obliged to shift from a reliance on its moral prestige to an increasing reliance on naked force. Wartime and postwar dangers seemed to give the balance of power at Chungking to those persons or groups who were most interested in the preservation of the regime at all costs. Faced with disaster, the whole regime relied on its organizers, as Chiang relied on the Ch'en brothers. Unfortunately the organizers were those who, through loyalty or personal ambition, placed the fortunes of the regime above all other considerations, including those of principle. Men who believed in secret police, thought control, and suppression of

opposition gained an ascendancy. This produced government action, like the punishment of critics, not justifiable in principle but based purely on force. The result was to antagonize formerly loyal elements. This weakened the regime. This increasing weakness being perceived, further reliance was placed upon force.

Only some such theory can explain the repeated acts by which the Kuomintang right wing lost the support of the intellectual and professional classes. Time after time government use of force against intellectuals served only to weaken its position among them. The public humiliation and beating of demonstrating students, who were mostly non-Communist, turned them toward Communism. In this way, the advocates of force obliged the government to rely on nothing else. Party dictatorship, while not an absolute power, became absolutely corrupted.

This corruption of the holders of Kuomintang power consisted in their sacrificing the general welfare to their own interest as a political group. By a more democratic rural program the Kuomintang could have competed against Communism at any time since 1927. After enveloping and expelling the Communists from Kiangsi in 1935 they sought to make it a model province but were unable to create a dynamic peasant movement. After the united front in 1937 the Kuomintang soon came to a turning point. Mass mobilization in the war of resistance was arousing the country and through it the Communists were extending their influence. The Kuomintang faced the alternative of competing directly with the Communists by encouraging mass resistance through social revolution, or fighting on two fronts against foreign invasion and domestic revolt at the same time. About 1938 they chose the latter course. This obviously sprang from a deep bureaucratic distrust of mass movements and popular initiative, and an easily rationalized determination to retain power at any price. This attitude, however, conduced to the loss of that moral prestige which was still one of the necessary ingredients of power. More and more people became prepared to turn against the government.

By war's end in 1945 the CCP had created a dynamic centrally-controlled movement in its own areas and exerted a great attraction upon intellectuals in Free China. Having done less of the fighting against Japan than the Nationalist Government and having avoided the burdens of city government and modern services, it was prepared to bid for power in the countryside. Only at this point did it become an immediate and inescapable problem for United States policy.

My view of this controversial question is that the American capacity to influence the Chinese scene in the 1940's has been exaggerated. I do not believe that a subcontinent of half a billion or more people, still largely imbedded in their own immemorial culture, inaccessible for the most part except by footpath or sampan, can be controlled from outside. It is noteworthy that the Chinese Communist Party, created expressly as a tool for foreign influence, followed the guidance of the Comintern in the 1920's only to disaster. It began its rise to power only after its alien creed had been adapted and Sinicized under Mao Tse-tung.

The outcome in 1949 showed, not that Soviet aid had been greater than American, but that the Chinese Communists had been able to mobilize and utilize the potentialities of revolution while the Nationalists had not. The Communist victory also showed that over a period of thirty years the American influence on China had not contributed to the organization of political power in an American fashion as effectively as the Soviet influence had contributed to its organization in a Soviet fashion. We had no Comintern. Behind our lack of a conspiratorial revolutionary apparatus lay the more general lack of any philosophy or method for forced-draft economic development and political collec-

tivism. Considering the suffering that rapid modernization of any sort was bound to bring upon the Chinese people, we need not entirely regret our inability to be China's model for the brutal task of remaking and industrializing her ancient society in the shortest possible time.

My answer to the imponderable question, Could we have saved China from Communism? is: Not without an utterly different approach prior to 1944; not at all thereafter. By the time we began to try, it was already too late.

In explaining China's modern history, the chief alternative to the traditional Chinese pattern is, of course, a traditional Western one. Where the Chinese pattern was cyclical, the Western view of history is based on the idea of linear progress (the two can be combined in a spiral). . . .

If one follows this Western-type pattern of unilinear social change in modern China, one may imperceptibly work one's historical interpretation around to the entirely false conclusion that Chinese Communism represents the inevitable current phase of China's modernization.

This would be just as simple-minded as to conclude that it is merely another in a long succession of dynasties. Neither view seems to me adequate.

In actual fact, of course, historical trends seldom develop in straight lines and Mao Tse-tung's being in power today depends on at least two particular circumstances among others: first, that Japan attacked and destroyed the more modern area of Kuomintang China; second, that Chiang Kai-shek, indomitable and uninstructable, developed in his long years on the mainland no rural reconstruction program such as has now been achieved on Taiwan. Peking naturally contends that historical necessity made Japan aggressive and Chiang blind to agrarian reform, but this hindsight overlooks the fact that historical trends are no one's monopoly and may be ridden by alternative power groups.

SUGGESTIONS FOR ADDITIONAL READING

Material on and concerning the defeat of the Kuomintang on the mainland are voluminous. Only a selected list of sources in Western languages is suggested here.

Two brief surveys of China's recent history are Victor Purcell's *The Rise of Modern China* (London: Routledge and Kegan, Paul, 1962), which is distinctly sympathetic to Communist China; and David Nelson Rowe's *Modern China: A Brief History* (Anvil, 1959), which is sympathetic to the Kuomintang; the latter includes twenty-two documents. A fuller political account is O. Edmund Clubb's *Twentieth Century China* (New York: Columbia University Press, 1964). Earl H. Pritchard's article entitled "Political Ferment in China, 1911–1951" appears in *The Annals of the American Academy of Political and Social Sciences* for September 1959 in a symposium, "Report on China," edited by Arthur H. Steiner. Another brief survey of article length is Mary C. Wright's "Modern China in Transition, 1900–1950" in *The Annals* for January 1959 under the general heading of "Contemporary China and the Chinese," edited by Howard L. Boorman. These two articles, useful in themselves, serve as introduction to more specialized topics on contemporary China.

Chinese Communist studies in the English language of China's modern history include Hu Sheng, *Imperialism and Chinese Politics* (Peking: Foreign Languages Press, 1955); Ho Kan-chih, *A History of the Modern Chinese Revolution* (Peking: Foreign Languages Press, 1959); and Chen Po-ta, *Notes on Ten Years of Civil War (1927–1936)* (Peking: Foreign Languages Press, 1954). Hu Sheng covers the period from the Opium War to 1924; Ho Kan-chih begins with the May 4th Movement of 1919; and Chen's book comprises the lectures he delivered in Yenan in the spring of 1944.

Some of the authors in this volume have expressed variants of their interpretations on the Kuomintang debacle. Ch'ien Tuan-sheng, in *The Government and Politics of China* (Cambridge: Harvard University Press, 1950) avers that the Chinese people must have "freedom from want" and "freedom from fear." Reference may also be made to two American statements: Dean Acheson's pronouncement of 1945 on the United States policy toward China, reprinted in U. S. Senate Joint Armed Services and Foreign Relations Committee, *Hearings on the Military Situation in the Far East*, 82nd Congress, 1st session, 1951, pp. 1838–57; and John S. Service, "Policies of the Chinese Communists Affecting Their Attitudes Toward the Soviet Union and the United States," in U. S. Senate Committee on Foreign Relations, *Hearings on the State Department Employee Loyalty Investigation*, 81st Congress, 2nd session, 1950, pp. 1364–68. Michael Lindsay's assessment of the military situation in China also appears in "Communist Against the Kuomintang, Which Side Can Win?" *Fabian Quarterly*, June 1947, pp. 25–31. A. Doak Barnett's *Communist China in Perspective* (New York: Frederick A. Praeger, Publisher, 1962) analyzes the historical forces contributing to the rise of the Chinese Communists and the fall of the Nationalists.

Several other interpretations of the Kuomintang debacle likewise represent important segments of the public opinion. Theodore Hsi-En Chen, "The Communist Victory in China," *World Affairs Interpreter*, January 1950, pp. 369–89, and Earl Swisher, "The Intellectuals' Dilemma on China Policy," *Social Science*, April 1954, pp. 67–74, are two brief, dispassionate accounts of the political, economic, military, and international factors in China immediately preceding the turnover. Chow Ching-wen, *Ten Years of Storm* (New York:

Holt, Rinehart & Winston, 1960), tells feelingly the reason for which many of the Chinese liberals became pro-Communist under the Kuomintang rule. Peter S. H. Tang, "Stalin's Role in the Communist Victory in China," *American Slavic and East European Review,* XIII (1954), 375–88, concurs with Hu Shih in believing that "Stalin's development of tactics for Mao had more influence on the course of events than is commonly supposed." Owen Lattimore, in *The Situation in Asia* (Boston: Little, Brown & Co., 1950), chapter 4, attributes the Kuomintang fall to economic wastefulness and administrative inefficiency born of the party's "feudal" mentality. Nathaniel Peffer, "Chinese Communist: Epoch or Episode?" *Yale Review,* XXXIX, No. 1 (September 1949), pp. 23–38, sees the "superficial" veneers of modernization in the Kuomintang's programs. Franz Michael, "The Fall of China," *World Politics,* VIII, No. 2 (January 1956), 296–306, expresses the view that "the fall of China to the Communists was the result of the collapse of a civilization and an ensuing chaos in which the attempts at reestablishing order, interrupted by the war, were too weak to stem the Communist tide." George C. Marshall's report of January 7, 1947, to President Truman, in *United States Relations with China,* pp. 686–88, identified political extremism and partisan distrust as causes of China's disorder. He urged the formation of a representative government composed of all "liberal" elements.

Chinese Communist interpretation is cogently presented by Chen Po-ta in *Stalin and the Chinese Revolution* (Peking: Foreign Languages Press, 1953), and *Mao Tse-tung on the Chinese Revolution* (Peking: Foreign Languages Press, 1953). Li Fu-jen, a leader of the National Salvation Movement in the 1930's and subsequently a Trotskyite wrote "The Kuomintang Faces Its Doom," *Fourth International,* X, No. 2 (February 1949), pp. 35–40, and "China: A World Power," *Fourth International,* XII, No. 1 (January–February, 1951), pp. 8–12. In the former article, he makes the

interesting nationalist-qua-internationalist statement:

> We can readily admit . . . that Mao Tse-tung and his leading henchmen are "stooges" of Moscow. With scrupulous fidelity they have geared their policies to every twist and turn of the Kremlin line for twenty years and more . . . . But when you have designated these dyed-in-the-wool Stalinists as stooges of the Kremlin, you have disclosed only a part of their political physiognomy, and not the most important part at that. In addition to being Stalin's agents, Mao and his cohorts are the leaders of a mighty, indigenous mass movement, the rebellious peasantry which constitutes more than 80 percent of the Chinese nation.

American opinion critical of the Kuomintang government is reflected in Lawrence K. Rosinger, "China in Ferment," *Foreign Policy Reports,* January 1, 1947, pp. 242–51; and T. A. Bisson, "China's Part in a Coalition War," *Far Eastern Survey,* July 14, 1943. Representative of the American "right" critical of the American government are Freda Utley, *The China Story* (Chicago: Henry Regnery Co., 1951; Great Debate Book, 1962); Walter H. Judd, "What Is the Truth About China? The Great Moral Decision of Chiang Kai-shek and the Chinese People," *Vital Speeches,* XI, No. 16 (June 1, 1945), 490–501; Patrick J. Hurley, "Causes of America's Failure in China," *Congressional Records,* Vol. 95, Part 12, 81st Congress, 1st session, 1949, pp. A1344–45; William C. Bullitt, "A Report to the American People on China," *Life,* October 13, 1947, pp. 35, 139–54; and Alfred Kohlberg, "Who Is Responsible for China's Tragedy?" *China Monthly,* December 1949, pp. 242–45, 250–51.

Many of the foreign correspondents in China in the forties were disillusioned with the Kuomintang regime. Having witnessed the lack of social purpose and political vigor in the Kuomintang areas, they were often attracted to the effective United Front programs and the apparently moderate attitudes of the Chinese Communists.

The first and most outstanding report among these eyewitness accounts is Edgar Snow's *Red Star Over China* (New York: Random House, 1938; Black Cat Book, 1961). His *Random Notes on Red China, (1936–1945)* (Cambridge: Harvard University Press, 1957) supplements the earlier work. Other accounts favorable to the Communists are Gunther Stein, *The Challenge of Red China* (New York: McGraw-Hill, 1945); Harrison Forman, *Report from Red China* (New York: Henry Holt, 1945); Jack Belden, *China Shakes the World* (New York: Harper, 1949); Jean-Jacques Brieux, *La Chine, du nationalisme au communisme* (Paris: Editions du Seuil, 1950); and Agnes Smedley, *Battle Hymn of China* (New York: Knopf, 1945). Israel Epstein, *The Unfinished Revolution in China* (Boston: Little, Brown, 1947), describes in great detail the economic and political developments in both the Kuomintang and Communist areas. Now a Chinese citizen and editor of the Foreign Languages Press in Peking, Epstein wrote *From Opium War to Liberation* (Peking: New World Press, 1956) without departing from the orthodox party line. Freda Utley's *The China Story*, already cited, is a hysterical warning against alleged Communist infiltration and influence in the American government, although in the early years of the war the author seemed to share the general, favorable attitude toward the United Front policy. In *China at War* (London: Faber and Faber, 1939), Miss Utley speaks kindly of her fellow correspondents such as Smedley and Belden, but her book *Last Chance in China* (New York: Bobbs-Merrill, 1947), already indicates her tendency toward the "China lobby" position. Lynn and Amos Landman, *Profile of Red China* (New York: Simon & Schuster, 1951), is a report of their observations in China from mid-1948 to mid-1950. George Moorad, *Lost Peace in China* (New York: Dutton, 1949), is in support of the "moral" cause of the Kuomintang, although he is equally vehement in his denunciation of government corruption.

The best reportage on life and conditions in the Kuomintang areas includes Theodore H. White and Annalee Jacoby, *Thunder Out of China* (New York: William Sloane Associates, 1946; Apollo, 1961); Graham Peck, *Two Kinds of Time* (Boston: Houghton Mifflin, 1950); and Robert Guillain, *600 Million Chinese,* translated by Mervyn Savill (New York: Criterion, 1957), chapter 2.

K. M. Panikkar was Indian Ambassador to China from 1948 to 1952; his *In Two Chinas: Memoirs of A Diplomat* (London: Allen & Unwin, 1955) is an impassive account of personal experiences and impressions. Derk Bodde, *Peking Diary: A Year of Revolution* (New York: Henry Schuman, Inc., 1950), is a sensitive depiction of day-to-day events in Peking, where the author spent the critical year of 1948–49. Robert Payne, *China Awake* (New York: Dodd, Mead, 1947) contains a poignant description of university life under the Kuomintang during 1944–46. Ralph and Nancy Lapwood, long-time British missionary teachers in China and residents in Peking in 1948–52, give a generally sympathetic account of the Communist regime in *Through the Chinese Revolution* (London: Spalding & Levy, 1954). Maria Yen (pseud.), *The Umbrella Garden: A Picture of Student Life in Red China* (New York: Macmillan, 1954) gives a lively depiction of student responses to the Communist rise to power. Liu Shaw-tong, *Out of Red China* (New York: Duell, Sloane & Pearce, 1953) provides helpful insight into the Communist takeover of China. Otto B. Van der Sprenkel, Robert Guillain and Michael Lindsay, who were in China during the takeover period, write of the sentiments and hopes then current in China in *New China: Three Views* (London: Turnstile Press, 1950). A. M. Dunlap, a resident of forty-one years in Peking and Shanghai, tells of the Communist takeover and initial rule in *Behind the Bamboo Curtain: The Experiences of An American Doctor in China* (Washington D. C.: Public Affairs Press, 1956), based principally upon his letters from Shanghai from April 1949 to October 1952. Chiang Mon-lin, Hu Shih's predecessor as Chancellor of the National Peking University, reminisces in *Tides from the West* (New Haven: Yale University Press, 1947).

Economic conditions are studied by D. S. Paauw, "Kuomintang and Economic Stagnation, 1928–1937," *Journal of Asian Studies*, February 1957, pp. 213–20; C. D. Campbell and G. C. Tullock, "Hyperinflation in China, 1937–49," *Journal of Political Economy* (1954), pp. 236–45; and Chou Shun-hsin, *The Chinese Inflation, 1937–1949* (New York: Columbia University Press, 1963). Arthur N. Young, Financial Adviser to the Kuomintang government from 1929 to 1947, has written *China and the Helping Hand, 1937–1945* (Cambridge: Harvard University Press, 1963), a study of China's financial, economic and international affairs.

For military situations and related aspects, reference may be made to Lionel-Max Chassin, *La Conquête de la Chine par Mao Tse-tung (1945–1949)* (Paris: Payot, 1952); General Henry Casseville, *De Chiang Kai Shek a Mao Tse Tung (Chine 1927–1950)* (Paris: Charles-Lavauzelle, 1950); and General David Barr's report of early 1949 on operational advice given to Chiang Kai-shek, as quoted in the *United States Relations with China*, pp. 325–38. George E. Taylor, *The Struggle for North China* (New York: International Secretariat, Institute of Pacific Relations, 1940) describes the resistance against Japan of Communist-organized Border Region Governments. Michael Lindsay, "The North China Front: A Study of Chinese Guerrillas in Action," *Amerasia*, March 31, 1944, pp. 100–10, and April 14, 1944, pp. 117–25, gives a parallel account on the same subject. Claire and William Band, *Two Years with the Chinese Communists* (New Haven: Yale University Press, 1948), is the personal account of a Yenching professor and his wife, who made their way from Peking in December, 1941, and, after traveling at leisurely pace through

Communist territories, left Yenan for Chungking in January 1944. Agnes Smedley recounts her experience with the Communist 8th Route Army in its formative days in *China Fights Back* (New York: Vanguard, 1938). Communist military tactics and organization are dealt with in Samuel B. Griffith, *Mao Tse-tung on Guerrilla Warfare* (New York: Frederick A. Praeger Inc., 1961), a translation, with introduction, of what is believed to be Mao's *Yu Chi Chan (Guerrilla Warfare)*; Robert B. Rigg, *Red China's Fighting Hordes* (Harrisburg, Pennsylvania: Military Service Publishing Co., 1952); and most recently in Edgar O'Ballance, *The Red Army of China: A Short History* (London: Faber & Faber, 1962).

Communist sources on military situations include Chu Teh, *On the Battlefronts of the Liberated Areas* (Peking: Foreign Languages Press, 1952), a military report to the 7th Congress of the CCP on April 25, 1945; Chu Teh, "On the Defeat of Chiang Kai-shek: Wall Street Puppet," *Political Affairs* (New York), August 1951, pp. 38–47; and Liao Kai-lung, *From Yenan to Peking: The Chinese People's War of Liberation from Reconstruction to First Five-Year Plan* (Peking: Foreign Languages Press, 1954). Russian sources include V. I. Glunin, *Tret'ya Grazhdanskaya Revolyutsionnaya Voina v Kitae (1946–1949) — Ocherk Politicheskoi Istorii* [The Third Revolutionary Civil War in China (1946–1949) — A Study of Political History] (Moscow: Izdatel'stvo Vostochnoi Literatury, 1958); and M. F. Iur'ev, ed., *Tret'ya Grazhdanskaya Revolyutsionnaya Voina v Kitae* (Moscow Voenizdat, 1957).

On Kuomintang politics, the most penetrating and comprehensive study is Ch'ien Tuan-sheng, *The Government and Politics of China*, cited above. Harley F. MacNair, *China in Revolution: An Analysis of Politics and Militarism under the Republic* (Chicago: University of Chicago Press, 1931), analyzes the fragmented political structure in China and tells of the kind of chaotic warlord autonomy that the Kuomintang had to cope with. Two different appraisals of the Kuomintang government, no doubt reflective of the time of writing, are Paul M. A. Linebarger's *The China of Chiang Kai-shek* (Boston: World Peace Foundation, 1941), and Lawrence K. Rosinger's *China's Wartime Politics, 1937–44* (Princeton: Princeton University Press, 1945) and *China's Crisis* (New York: Alfred A. Knopf, Inc., 1945). *China Handbook, 1937–45* (New York: Macmillan Co., 1947) by the Chinese Ministry of Information, with a 1946 supplement, is a comprehensive official survey of the major developments in the eight years of war against Japan. Robert C. North, *Kuomintang and Chinese Communist Elites* (Stanford: Stanford University Press, 1952), shows the remarkable stableness of the Kuomintang leadership in office.

Hollington K. Tong's *Chiang Kai-shek, Soldier and Statesman* (2 volumes, Shanghai: China Publishing Co., 1937) is an authorized biography; his revised edition *Chiang Kai-shek* (Taipei: China Publishing Co., 1953) in one volume is a completely rewritten work. Equally eulogistic is Emily Hahn's *Chiang Kai-shek: An Unauthorized Biography* (Garden City: Doubleday, 1955). Somewhat more critical are H. H. Chang, *Chiang Kai-shek: Asia's Man of Destiny* (Garden City: Doubleday, 1944), and Robert Berkov, *Strong Man of China: The Story of Chiang Kai-shek* (Boston: Houghton Mifflin, 1938), both being political biographies. Most revealing of Chiang Kai-shek's philosophy is his *China's Destiny,* written in 1943; it was not rendered into English until 1947, in the authorized translation by Wang Chung-hui (New York: Macmillan Co., 1947) and another by Philip Jaffe (New York: Roy, 1947). The Jaffe edition, with notes and commentary, also includes Chiang's *Chinese Economic Theory,* a work equally revealing of the author's nationalistic predilection. Representative of Chiang's views on a wider range of subjects is *The Collected Wartime Messages of Generalissimo Chiang Kai-shek, 1937–*

1945 (2 volumes, New York: John Day Co., 1946). Chiang's *Chapters on National Fecundity, Social Welfare, Education, and Health and Happiness* (Taipei: China Cultural Service, n. d.) is his supplement to Sun Yat-sen's unfinished lectures on the Principle of People's Livelihood and his claim to Sun's legacy. Sun Yat-sen's *Three People's Principles* was best tranlated by Frank W. Price and L. T. Chen in *San Min Chu I* (Shanghai: The Commercial Press, 1927), since reproduced in both complete and abridged forms by Kuomintang government publishing agencies.

Chinese Communism and the role of the Soviet Union in the 1920's have been studied in great detail in a number of scholarly works. Benjamin I. Schwartz, *Chinese Communism and the Rise of Mao* (Cambridge: Harvard University Press, 1951), is the first major survey of the intra-party ideological debate in the 20's and is to be read with Conrad Brandt, Benjamin I. Schwartz and John K. Fairbank, *A Documentary History of Chinese Communism* (Cambridge: Harvard University Press, 1952). M. N. Roy, *Revolution and Counter-Revolution in China* (Calcutta: Renaissance, 1946), is valuable for the personal experiences of the author as a Comintern agent in Wuhan during the crucial year of 1927. C. Martin Wilbur and Julie Lien-ying How, *Documents on Communism, Nationalism, and Soviet Advisers in China, 1918–1927* (New York: Columbia University Press, 1956), is a study important for the authentication and interpretation of the documents seized in the 1927 raid on the Soviet embassy by the Peking government of Chang Tso-lin. For Soviet involvement in China, there are four outstanding volumes: Allen S. Whiting, *Soviet Politics in China, 1917–1924* (New York: Columbia University Press, 1953); Conrad Brandt, *Stalin's Failure in China, 1924–27* (Cambridge: Harvard University Press, 1958); Xenia J. Eudin and Robert C. North, *Soviet Russia and the East, 1920–1927: A Documentary Survey* (Stanford: Stanford University Press, 1957); and for a later period, Charles B. McLane, *Soviet Policy and the Chinese Communists, 1931–1946* (New York: Columbia University Press, 1958). Hu Chiao-mu, *Thirty Years of the Communist Party of China* (Peking: Foreign Languages Press, 1951, 1959), is a significant official account.

Three authoritative studies of American policy toward China during and after the Pacific War are: Herbert Feis, *The China Tangle: The American Effort in China from Pearl Harbor to the Marshall Mission* (Princeton: Princeton University Press, 1953); Charles F. Romanus and Riley Sunderland, *United States Army in World War II: China-Burma-India Theater* (3 volumes, Washington D. C.: Office of the Chief of Military History, Department of the Army, 1952–59); and Tang Tsou, *America's Failure in China, 1941–50.* Tang Tsou, "The Historians and the Generals," *Pacific Historical Review,* February, 1962, pp. 41–48, on General Albert C. Wedemeyer; and Don Lohbeck, *Patrick J. Hurley* (Chicago: Henry Regnery Co., 1956), discuss the political complexities in China and the political dilemmas faced by these two dedicated public servants. The Yalta Conference and its several aspects have been the subject of a number of personal accounts, scholarly studies and popular interpretations; only two need be mentioned here: Richard F. Fenno, Jr., ed., *The Yalta Conference* (Boston: D. C. Heath, 1955) in the *Problems in American Civilization* series; and John L. Snell, ed., *The Meaning of Yalta* (Baton Rouge: Louisiana State University Press, 1956). America's China policy in the post-World War II period was re-opened to examination in several Congressional hearings, among which are: U. S. Senate Committee on Armed Service, *Hearings on the Nomination of General George C. Marshall to Be Secretary of Defense,* 81st Congress, 2nd session, 1950; U. S. Senate Committee on Judiciary, *Hearings on the Institute of Pacific Relations,* 82nd Congress, 1st and 2nd sessions, 1951–52; and *Hearings on State Department Employee Loyalty Investigation* and *Hearings on the Military Situation in the Far East,* cited above.

A number of helpful bibliographies on modern China have appeared in recent years, with useful notes and commentaries. John K. Fairbank's *Bibliographical Guide to Modern China: Works in Western Languages* (Cambridge: Committee on International and Regional Studies, Harvard University, 1948) has been followed among others by Yuan Tung-li, *China in Western Literature: A Continuation of Cordier's Bibliotheca Sinica* (New Haven: Far Eastern Publications, Yale University, 1958); American University Field Staff, *A Select Bibliography: Asia, Africa, Eastern Europe, Latin America* (New York: AUFS, 1960), with supplements; and Charles O. Hucker, *China: A Critical Bibliography* (Tucson: University of Arizona Press, 1962). The Sections on China in the American Historical Association's *Guide to Historical Literature* (New York: Macmillan Co., 1961), are prepared by Earl H. Pritchard, T. H. Tsien, and Charles S. Gardner. Richard Harris, *Modern China* (London: Cambridge University Press, 1961) is a 32-page annotated bibliography prepared for the National Book League in England. The Service Center for Teachers of History of the American Historical Association has published two thoughtful bibliographical essays: Allan B. Cole's *Forty Years of Chinese Communism: Selected Readings with Commentary* (1962) and Charles O. Hucker's *Chinese History: A Bibliographical Review* (1958).

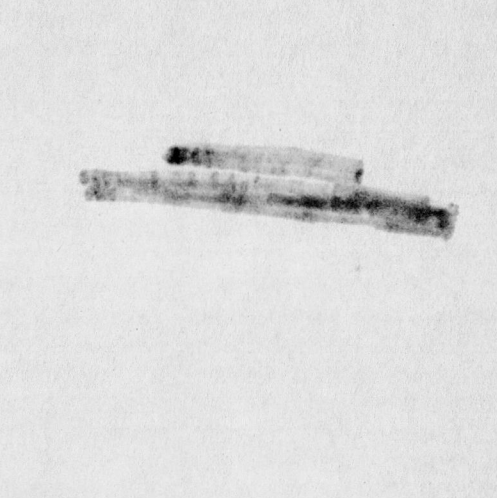